ACE OF CADS

THE MONROE OWSLEY STORY

CHASE LLOYD

Cover photograph by Clarence Sinclair Bull. Scan and cover design by Chase Lloyd.

Formatted in Vellum.

ACKNOWLEDGMENTS

Ace of Cads wouldn't have happened without several wonderful authors, classic cinema fans, institutions, and an entourage of encouraging readers.

Much gratitude to Cliff Aliperti, Stephanie Jones, Scott O'Brien, Lawrence J. Quirk, William Schoell, André Soares, and Larry Swindell for their excellent writings on Old Hollywood legends.

Much gratitude to Alamy, Library of Congress, Maryland Room at Talbot County Free Library, Media History Digital Library, fultonhistory.com, and newspapers.com for providing valuable research resources and materials for the book.

Much gratitude to my readers and friends who donated their time, energy, and money toward making the book possible. Every single one of you are responsible for preserving Monroe Owsley's legacy. I cannot thank you enough for helping me.

INTRODUCTION

One early morning in February, I posted a little joke on social media.

Book written by a professional researcher: This person's death remains mysterious.

Me, who just learned of this person's existence one page ago: I bet I can solve this mystery.

Make the joke and forget about this guy, I had thought then. But I couldn't move on. In Lawrence J. Quirk's *Fasten Your Seat Belts: The Passionate Life of Bette Davis,* the author briefly discusses a film and stage actor that Davis had co-starred with in 1933's *Ex-Lady*. This actor passed away in 1937 at only thirty-six years of age. Quirk—who had peppered the pages with rumors of homosexual seductions, alcohol and drug use, and gambling—noted the circumstances of the actor's death were mysterious and insinuated a possible cover up.

That book was published in 1990. It's 2024 now. Is this eighty-seven-year-old death still mysterious?

What happened to Monroe Owsley?

As of this writing, a cursory look at Wikipedia reveals just the basics. His date of birth and place, his start in acting with stock theater troupes that turned into a Broadway and film career, and his death date. IMDb has a more detailed description (with less than glowing adjectives), but it's also quite brief. Owsley's biography on Turner Classic Movies's website is the most concise with a few titles listed and his death date. Nothing that reveals anything about his personality or ambitions.

With no books published about Owsley and only a few posts devoted to him on Old Hollywood blogs, my next step was to look for contemporaneous articles about the actor. After a few clumsy searches through various digital archives, it quickly became clear to me this investigation would be more challenging than I had initially thought.

Owsley had passed away the same day as the much more famous actress Jean Harlow, who had succumbed to complications of kidney failure at the age of twenty-six. Where Owsley's death would get a few paragraphs at most in newspapers, there were full pages dedicated to Harlow.

In addition to the limited coverage devoted to Owsley, there were conflicting details about his death. Some papers, like *The New York Times,* reported Owsley was on a train from Los Angeles to San Francisco when a heart attack struck him. Other papers, like *Los Angeles Daily News,* claimed that Owsley passed away in Belmont Hospital while en route to Hollywood. *Santa Ana Journal* reported that Owsley had been visiting friends in San Mateo after attending the Golden Gate Bridge opening.

Other conflicting details in Owsley's obituaries include his age and the actual date he passed, but those are easier to confirm in the digital age. It does, however, make it more confusing to decide which newspapers had more accurate reports. Almost none of them seemed to have had much to go on. *Santa Ana Journal* in particular noted that "details of his death were lacking."

Only one newspaper, *The San Mateo Times,* pressed for the

truth about Owsley's death. Any other journalistic interest in the case might have been pushed aside for the more lurid story surrounding Jean Harlow's death. Harlow was a popular leading actress regarded as a sex symbol with numerous previous (and very public) tragedies in her life. It's easy to see why the news prioritized her story over Owsley's.

But in doing my research on this obscure actor, I can't help wondering if the day he died matters much at all. Very few mentions have been published about him since his death. Almost none of his costars mentioned him in their memoirs. No one in the public eye seemed to miss him.

Was there a reason for this? Was he not worth missing? Or—if he truly had been a queer man with substance use disorders—was he not the right type of person the conservative Hays Code era of Hollywood wanted to be missed?

Who was Monroe Owsley?

CHAPTER ONE

The United States of America was in the midst of great change in the year 1900. Though moving pictures had been invented, Hollywood didn't exist yet. The newfound automobile industry was growing by leaps and bounds. Women fought for the right to vote. Racial tensions were thick in America, especially in the South, where deadly riots swept through Louisiana that summer. The Great War and Prohibition were mere years away from further shaping the country—and Monroe Owsley.

Monroe "Buck" Righter Owsley was born on August 11, 1900 in Atlanta, Georgia. He was the third child for Harry Monroe Owsley, a manufacturing executive, and the first child for Gertrude "Gertie" Alice Righter, a concert singer.

Harry M. married Ida Matthews in 1880. Their wedding was described in *The Atlanta Constitution* as "an ocean of rare pleasure."[1] They had two children together—Gertrude McVeigh, born in 1881, and Harry Albert, born in 1883. Ida passed away sometime in 1892. Details about her, her life, and her death are lacking.

Before the end of 1893, Harry M. married Gertie. Gertie was

a light opera soprano who received a fair amount of attention in Atlanta and St. Louis for her performances. One of her notable roles includes the part of Serpolette in *The Chimes of Normandy*. She was described as "a pretty young matron with a beautiful voice" and "a wonderfully clever actress."[2]

Gertie Owsley in the St. Louis Post-Dispatch, *1908. (courtesy newspapers.com)*

In 1903, Gertie gave birth to another child, a daughter named after Gertie's mother. Tragically, Abbie Lettela Owsley passed away a few months later from an illness.

Despite the age gap between Monroe Owsley and his older siblings, the whole family was close. His sister married A. Scott Ledbetter in 1902 and gave birth to a son, John, the following year. Sometime shortly after that, Scott abandoned his family and married another woman in 1906, leaving Gertrude to raise John alone. Curiously, in the 1910 census, Gertrude still claimed him as her husband—and Scott's obituary in 1925 claimed she had died.[3] Until her second marriage in 1922, Gertrude lived with either Harry Albert or her parents and "Buck."

"Buck" was the best man for his brother's wedding in 1918 to Katherine Nichols. Their wedding was small and private due to the war going on at the time. Katherine was a young woman from Yonkers, New York who pursued several artistic passions through her life. She enjoyed music, held exhibits for her paintings, and wrote poems that were published in El Paso, Texas newspapers and *Good Housekeeping* magazine.

In 1919, Gertrude's son passed away during a duck hunting trip. John Ledbetter was sixteen at the time. He died trying to saving his friend, fifteen-year-old Raymond Iszard. They passed from either exposure or drowning, and it took time for their bodies to be found. The boys were buried together. After that horrific accident, Owsley became his sister's travel companion for several months.

With so much heartache and death in the family, including Harry and Gertie's parents all passing away by 1909, it's easy to see why the Owsleys were close to each other.

There were multiple mentions through the years of the Owsleys visiting each other or vacationing together. Gertie, in particular, was never far from her son during his stage years. In 1930, a humorous article emerged where Harry M. offered five thousand dollars for his son to finish his shooting schedule in time to be home for Christmas.[4] Later in Owsley's film career, his parents moved out to California to be closer to him. At the end of Owsley's life, he was living with his brother and sister-in-law in Santa Monica.

Harry and Gertie moved around with their young son while "Buck" grew up. The various places they lived in included El Paso, Hartford, New York, and Philadelphia. As a teenager, Owsley attended schools across Connecticut and Pennsylvania, including Loomis Institute, Bristol High School, and West Philadelphia High School. Future Hollywood actress Jeanette MacDonald was also a student at West Philadelphia, but she and Owsley didn't know each other at the time.

Owsley grew up comfortably. His family was quite well off, and "Buck" could be found donating modest sums of money to

Christmas charities in his youth. During his school years, he pursued athletic activities like baseball, football, and track. Owsley had some aspirations to play baseball professionally, but that didn't happen, for whatever reason. His 1918 draft registration card notes an issue with his spine, which might have kept him from pursuing sports further.

Or maybe his interest in acting outweighed athletics.

Owsley knew at an early age that he wanted to get into acting, though he would later claim he couldn't remember why or when. It was just "one of those things."[5] *El Paso Herald-Post* reported that he had run around with the El Paso theater set during his brief duration in Texas as a juvenile. [6]*The El Paso Times* noted that Owsley had trained a group of young people for a home talent show during his stay.[7]

Harry and Gertie, however, had other ambitions after Owsley completed high school. Acting was not seen as a serious profession back then, and the more conservative people considered it be an inherently immoral occupation. Owsley's parents wished for their son to stay away from the footlights and attend Yale.

He obeyed. Sort of.

During his preparations for Yale, Owsley joined ROTC and a fraternity, and he took a job at the *Public Ledger* in Philadelphia as a cub reporter. At the paper, he had many general assignments, but he also reviewed theatrical performances and shared backstage gossip. Owsley's other work included employment as a gas station attendant and driving Roamer cars for the luxury automobile manufacturer, Barley Motor Car Company.

Eventually, Owsley could no longer resist the call to acting—or perhaps he had been let go from the *Public Ledger*. Cameron Shipp at *The Charlotte News*[8] revealed a humorous story after Owsley's death about a time "Buck" had made a bad decision to slack off on his work. He had been assigned to cover a play, but he had seen the play some weeks prior in New York, so he wrote a long, critical piece and took the night off. His review appeared in the paper's morning issue—the same issue that covered the show's cancellation. The playhouse had been destroyed by a fire the previous night.

Either way, Owsley moved to New York City, home of America's biggest theater scene. While searching for acting gigs, he enrolled in a journalism course at Columbia University around 1921. During this phase, he lived in a theatrical boarding house on West 88th Street.

Owsley frequently escorted another boarder—emerging Broadway actress Ann Harding—around town. The pair would meet almost every night and enjoy a variety of artistic activities. Together, they attended movies and lectures, visited museums, and discussed books.

Another fellow boarder, Frank Easton, remarked in a June 1936 *Modern Screen* article[9] that Owsley had loved Harding, but she hadn't returned the feelings. "In fact, men didn't mean a great deal to her. She preferred friendship to romance—and Owsley was that friend." When Owsley and Easton moved to Columbia University's campus, they lost contact with Harding. Owsley and Harding would reunite several years later in Hollywood.

Somewhere around 1921, Owsley allegedly had a bit part in the silent film *Jim the Penman*, which starred Lionel Barrymore. In an interview with *The New Movie Magazine*, Owsley noted that Barrymore would later be his director in *Ten Cents a Dance.*[10] *Jim the Penman* is missing one of its reels, and it's not readily available to watch, so it's difficult to confirm if Owsley made it to the finished product.

After Columbia University, Owsley enrolled in the American Academy of Dramatic Arts. His classmates included future theater and film stars Spencer Tracy, Pat O'Brien, George Meeker, Charles Wagenheim, Kay Johnson, and Sterling

Holloway. O'Brien would eventually drop out from the course, but the others graduated together in March of 1923.

Owsley took a great interest in Tracy, according to biographer Larry Swindell.[11] Allegedly, Owsley looked down on most of his fellow classmates, but he found Tracy to be a better actor than himself. Owsley had enrolled at the academy to make connections, and he insisted he would help Tracy, who had not done any stage work in New York before.

Though Tracy found Owsley cynical (Owsley believed only a few Broadway offices could make stars out of their actors), the pair spent time together outside of their course activities. Tracy was poor, but "Buck" had money, and the latter didn't seem to mind having the former spend it with him sometimes. Owsley had tips on fixed races, speakeasies, and "girls in Brooklyn with liberal ideas."

Owsley was true to his word about getting Tracy his break in theater. Owsley was offered two walk-on roles in a play at nearly the same time, and he passed the word along about one of them to Tracy. Soon enough, Tracy had his Broadway debut in Karel Capek's *R.U.R.* as a nonspeaking robot, even though he didn't really know what a robot was at the time. Tracy was soon able to get his roommate, O'Brien, to fill in as another robot.

The seniors at the academy put on a variety of short plays and scenes. Owsley received much attention for his acts, including two plays he had been in with his pal Tracy—Harley Granville-Barker's *The Marrying of Ann Leete* and Oscar Wilde's *The Importance of Being Earnest.*

During his tenure at the academy, Owsley had his first Broadway stage appearance in a mystery play written by Leonard Praskins and Ernest Pascal, *The Charlatan.*[12] His role was minor enough that his name didn't appear in reviews, but his being in the play was significant enough to be of note in future articles about him. Other plays he did around this time were Frederic S. Isham's *Three Live Ghosts* and Bayard Veller's *The Thirteenth Chair.*

Following graduation, Owsley landed a role in a touring tent show on the Redpath Chautauqua circuit.[13] He played the role of Ned Stephens in *The Meanest Man in the World.* Outdoor tent shows were at the height of their heyday in the 1920s, bringing relief to audiences who felt stifled in opera houses and theater venues in the days before central air conditioning.

The Meanest Man in the World went on tour for around one hundred and twenty performances during the late spring and summer of 1923. The three act comedy drama was written by Augustin MacHugh and based on a skit by Everett Ruskay. The story revolves around a soft-hearted, poor lawyer who decides to become the meanest man in the world in order to become successful. His attempts to be selfish are forgotten when he meets a pretty young woman facing legal troubles.

The grueling travel and constant work demanded a lot from Owsley, but he was up to the challenge. In fact, the experience made him more hungry for a Broadway career. He would later fondly reminisce about the touring days where he had to dart through the rain and mud in a white flannel costume from his dressing tent.[14]

Owsley returned to New York after the tent show and landed a role in *Merton of the Movies* in October 1923. The four act comedy had been a hit on Broadway and ran for nearly a full year. When Owsley joined the show, the production was getting ready to go on tour.

Merton of the Movies, based on a novel by Harry Leon Wilson and dramatized by George S. Kaufman and Marc Connelly, follows a small-town general store clerk who heads to Hollywood to make better pictures than the current screen dramas. The comedy both satirized the movie industry and painted it in a sympathetic light. It received much praise from critics during both its original stage run and its time on the road.

Owsley played the part of Kid Parker, but he also managed to beat thirty other applicants to get a secondary—and more prestigious—role as the understudy for leading man Glenn Hunter. Owsley was close friends with Hunter, but he also idolized him. The young actor had big ambitions of his own to wear the same crown as Hunter. *Merton of the Movies* had turned Hunter into a major stage star, and the success of the play prompted a screen version with Hunter. Unfortunately, the film is now considered lost.

Merton of the Movies spent ten weeks in Chicago at the end of 1923. It continued to tour through cities along the Subway Circuit during the spring of 1924. As the season came to a close, Owsley took a brief break from the stage and spent some time with his family.

A February 1924 article from *Hartford Courant*[15] suggests the possibility of another silent picture in Owsley's filmography. During his time with *Merton of the Movies,* Owsley was slated to "make his second appearance in the movies." The film would be made by Film Guild Productions, a studio that only produced movies starring Hunter. The studio folded sometime in 1924, and no pictures appear to have been released from them following the article's release. It's unclear if Owsley's "second appearance in the movies" acknowledges his bit role in *Jim the Penman.*

The name Monroe Owsley started appearing in newspapers again later in the summer. With Fritzi Brunette as the star and Warren Ashe in the cast, he appeared in a one act comedy in Sioux City, *Spring and the Moonlight.* The sketch centers a young woman choosing between two men, one rich, and one poor. "She chooses the poor one, which seemed to be all right."[16]

MON-
R O E
OWSLEY, son of Mr. and Mrs. H. M. Owsley of Highland Court hotel, understudy to Glenn Hunter in "Merton of the Movies," will play the leading juvenile role in "The Goose Hangs High," the New York success, which will start on the road in September.

(C) Unity Photo Co.

Portrait of Owsley featured in The Hartford Courant, *1924.*
(courtesy newspapers.com)

After the brief engagement, Owsley joined the Dramatists' Theater, Inc. production of Lewis Beach's *The Goose Hangs High.* The Dramatists' Theater, Inc. was a fairly new organization. Formed in 1923 by a small group of playwrights, *The Goose Hangs High* was their first production with James Forbes as the director. It had a successful run at the Bijou in New York before Owsley joined as part of the touring production.

The three act comedy went on tour in late September of 1924. Beach's story follows two self-sacrificing parents who have recently lost their income. Still, they're determined to keep up aristocratic appearances for their eldest son, who is soon to be married, and their twins, who attend an expensive college. When the children find out their parents' financial affairs are bleak, they work together with their grandmother to overcome the crisis and help their parents.

The play and its positive message about young adults received praises across multiple cities. *Buffalo Courier* described it as "intensely human."[17] Owsley played the artistic twin brother, Bradley Ingals, and received a modest amount of attention for his performance. After *The Goose Hangs High*, Owsley joined Fritzi Brunette and Warren Ashe again for another appearance in *Spring and the Moonlight*.

In late March 1925, the Stuart Walker Company announced four new repertory players that would alternate between Walker's companies in Cincinnati and Dayton, Ohio during the summer. The newcomers were Ralph Kellard, Rosalind Ivan, Reba Garden, and Monroe Owsley. Two more players, Mona Burns and Leonore Sorsby, were included in the augmentation the following week.

Stuart Walker had developed an interest in theater at an early age, thanks to a toy theater set his father had given to him as a child. Walker was one of the first producers to pioneer the apprentice system for training repertory players. His vision of building a company with many skilled actors instead of pushing for one star won him much prestige among theater-goers and much loyalty from his crew. He later became involved in Hollywood and saw many familiar faces he had worked with during his stock days.

Owsley's first show with Stuart Walker was Avery Hopwood

and David Gray's *The Best People*. The three act comedy marked the start of a strong season for the company with its quirky characters and flashy quips. Two grown children of a wealthy family wish to marry outside of their "class." At the heart of the story is a struggle between an older, conservative generation and a younger, free-spirited generation.

Owsley played the idealistic son of the aristocratic family, determined to marry a chorus girl. He received praise as Bertie Lenox, especially for pulling off "one difficult drunk scene."[18] This would be the first of many, many mentions for Owsley's ability to play drunk characters.

Owsley got to play someone a little different and a lot less aristocratic for his next role. He was cast as a fighter, Bully Boy Brewster, in Rida Johnson Young's four act play, *Little Old New York*. The play follows a young woman, Patricia O'Day (Lucile Nikolas), who must pose as her deceased brother in order to claim an inheritance. The prize fight Bully Boy participates in causes Patricia to reveal her identity. Owsley "distinguished himself and took applause with him on last exit."[19]

The third Stuart Walker vehicle of the season allowed Owsley to reprise his role as the son in *The Goose Hangs High*. Another member of the company, George Alison, also reprised his original role as the Ingals patriarch from the Dramatists' Theater Inc. tour.

During this production of *The Goose Hangs High*, a surprising announcement emerged. On April 27, 1925, *Dayton Daily News* reported the engagement of Monroe Owsley to Ziegfeld "Follies" girl, Yvonne Grey. The announcement mentioned that the romance had begun when the pair were cast members for *Merton of the Movies*.

However, on May 2, Grey denied the engagement and also denied any intentions to marry Owsley. The next day, Owsley issued his own statement in *Dayton Daily News*[20].

"I am glad that Miss Grey has denied the rumor of our

engagement. Though we have known each other for a long time and have been the best of friends for several years we are not and never have been engaged. When I was playing in 'The Goose Hangs High' on the road last autumn our engagement was announced in the New York newspapers. It is rather an odd coincidence that the second announcement should come when I am again appearing in 'The Goose Hangs High.'"

This researcher personally was unable to find evidence of a first engagement announcement, but that doesn't mean it didn't exist at some point.

Owsley continued with his statement, highlighting the prominent reason the engagement could never happen.

"Had we ever considered becoming engaged it would not take place for a long time, as Miss Grey has just been elevated to an important role in a new number which Mr. Ziegeld has only recently inserted in the Follies."

"She is, I think, one of the most talented and promising young musical comedy actresses in the country today. But as for being engaged,—well, that is all a mistake."

Oddly, later that summer, multiple newspapers across the country ran a large article devoted to explaining the engagement process for the Ziegfeld beauties. It notably highlighted that Grey had gone through the rigorous four stage process with Owsley, only to break it off at the end. "A special committee of the dressing rooms is going over the evidence on a strong suspicion that one or more of the preliminary stages was skimped."[21]

Whether the engagement was ever real remains a mystery.

After *The Goose Hangs High,* Stuart Walker put on Gilbert Emery's three act drama, *Tarnish*. Owsley was not named in any articles related to *Tarnish*. If he had a role, it was very minor.

Guy Bolton's *Chicken Feed,* a three act comedy, served as Stuart Walker's next Dayton presentation where Owsley had a named role. The play centers a rising concern of its time—

financial equality for housewives. At the urge of one of their daughters (Nell Bailey, played by Lucile Nikolas), two married women wish to get their husbands to either pay them a salary or divide the household income equally. Nell also has plans to marry a man who isn't very practical and focuses more on romance (Ralph Kellard's Danny Kester).

Owsley played Chester Logan, the young lawyer who's been in love with Nell for ages. He attempts to win her over, offering her the financial security and household help she vocally wants. Still, her heart remains with Danny.

The next play from the Dayton players was a three act mystery, Eleanor Robson and Harriet Ford's *In the Next Room,* adapted from a novel by Burton E. Stevenson. Two noiseless murders occur with no clues, and the mystery combines humor and suspense to thrill audiences. Owsley was named in the cast, but it is currently unknown which role he played.

After *In the Next Room,* Owsley traveled to Cincinnati. The company put on *The Best People* there, where Owsley reprised his role for the Cincinnati audience.

An article from May 24, 1925 noted that Owsley still remained interested in journalism at the time. He asked a local editor to give him some assignments during his stay just to "keep his hand in."[22]

The crew went back to Dayton in June and put on *Kiki,* André Picard's three act character study that had been a tremendous success on Broadway under David Belasco's direction. Though Owsley's role in the play is currently unknown, a picture of him grinning with a cigarette in his hand dominated *The Dayton Herald*'s Theaters section in anticipation of the play. The leads, Lucile Nikolas and Ralph Kellard, were well-received. The company's art director, Charles Elrod, was also praised for the Paris stage setting.

The following week, Owsley replaced Earle Larrimore in Lynn Starling's *Meet the Wife.* The three act comedy earned its laughs following Gertrude Lennox (Spring Byington), a woman who realizes she's inadvertently married to two men when her first husband returns after a sudden disappearance. So much attention was given to Byington in the newspapers that it makes it difficult to determine what role Owsley had. The enthusiasm shone toward Byington, however, makes this particular researcher wish they had seen the play.

Next, Owsley scored a scene-stealing role in a three act comedy written by Adelaide Matthews and Anne Nichols. *Just Married* accidentally brings two strangers with the identical name of Roberta Adams (Ralph Kellard and Lucile Nikolas) together. They end up sharing the same stateroom *and* the same bed on an ocean liner. Owsley played Johnny Walker who—with Regina Stanfiel as his wife—didn't say a single word during the play. The pair provided the biggest laughs by simply appearing at every exciting moment and walking really fast.

During that week, Owsley had an article devoted to him in *Dayton Daily News*.[23] "I never get the girl," he said.

"It is only occasionally that there is any love interest in the roles assigned [to] me, and when there is, someone else is always the fortunate one to step up just before the final curtain and claim the girl. Someday, sometime and somewhere I hope to get away from comedy roles long enough to have one real romantic part."

The *Dayton Daily News* article was just the first of Owsley's many public attempts to break away from typecasting. His desire to play romantic heroes would be expressed repeatedly throughout his Hollywood days.

Smilin' Through by Allan Langdon Martin (a pseudonym for Jane Cowl and Jane Murfin) was the next Stuart Walker Company production that Owsley was in. Though his role is currently unknown, the three act play with a prologue charmed its audiences. The story is about a young Irish woman who falls for the one man her adopted father opposes—the son of the man who stole his first love.

Grounds for Divorce, adapted by Guy Bolton from Hungarian playwright Ernest Vadja's original play, gave Owsley a part closer to what he wanted. The three act comedy centers a divorce lawyer (Ralph Kellard's Maurice Sorbier) who finds himself divorced after neglecting his wife, Denise (Lucile Nikolas). When he prepares for a second marriage, Denise returns, pretending to be married and wanting a divorce from her second husband so she can marry a third man. All of the charades were to win her first husband back.

The third man, ace Italian aviator Marchese Guido, was played by Owsley. The role of hopeful whirlwind lover won Owsley the most attention amongst his other parts during the summer with Stuart Walker. Though he got to flex some of his romance hero capabilities, the aviator would wind up without the woman he wanted.

Booth Tarkington's three act comedy, *Clarence,* was Owsley's last play with Stuart Walker, and it marked the end of the company's stock season. The story concerns a disabled soldier who becomes a family friend to a wealthy family whose matters have gone awry. Indications are that Owsley played the juvenile role, the family's son in love with a tutor, but this is not currently confirmed.

After *Clarence*'s run, Owsley returned to his family's home in Hartford for some rest. An article discussed the possibility of a trip into Canada and some motion picture work. Owsley had apparently had some negotiations with filmmaker Cecil B. DeMille, but the conversations ultimately didn't blossom into any actual movies from the Hollywood legend.

Owsley would not rest for long. By fall, he was back on stage. This time, to a larger audience.

He had attained a prominent role in a Broadway play.

CHAPTER TWO

In early November of 1925, news emerged that Monroe Owsley had signed with the Dramatists' Theater, Inc. to complete the cast for James Forbes's three act comedy drama, *Young Blood.* Owsley had been directed by Forbes in *The Goose Hangs High* the year before. It was Forbes's return as a playwright after involving himself with directing for the Dramatists' Theater, Inc. The Canadian playwright had received critical acclaim for *The Famous Mrs. Fair* back in 1919.

Young Blood shows the explosive struggle between a wealthy, indulgent father (Norman Trevor's Alan Dana) and his song (Eric Dressler's Alan, Jr.) after the son flunks out of college. Alan, Jr. gets involved in an affair with Louise (Florence Eldridge), the parlor maid who seeks to marry Alan Jr. for his fortune. Alan Jr. is saved from the gold digger when his neighbor and true love interest, Georgia Bissell (Helen Hayes), exposes Louise as a faker. Owsley played Georgia's brother, Sammy. Winston Lee was Owsley's understudy.

Years later, Owsley praised Hayes in a *New York Sun* article,[1] referring to her as one of the best actresses in the world. "She is marvelous to play with. She gives so much to the other actors. You find yourself giving a good performance too, playing up to hers. It's something an actress either has or hasn't—you can't explain it."

The play did performances in Rochester, New York and Pittsburgh, Philadelphia before officially opening at the Ritz Theatre (currently known as the Walter Kerr Theatre) in New York City on November 24.

Young Blood received mixed reviews, and the show was ultimately not quite up to Forbes's past work. It closed at the Ritz on January 23, 1926. A couple of days later, *Young Blood* opened at Princess Theatre in Chicago. The play ran for six weeks until March 6.

By April, Owsley returned to stock theater, this time with the Poli Players.[2]

The Poli Players, owned by theater magnate Sylvester Z. Poli, performed close to Owsley's Hartford home. He spent that spring and summer performing juvenile roles in Springfield, Massachusetts, less than an hour's drive from his parents. The company opened their season at Court Square on April 26 with *Easy Come, Easy Go*.

Owen Davis's three act comedy was still being shown on Broadway at the time, but Poli secured the rights to "pre-release" it before the play was available for general stock presentation. The story follows the hijinks of a reluctant thief and his more devious friend on the run from the police. The crooks end up meeting a millionaire and his vapid prospective son-in-law on their way to a sanitarium. The hero and unwilling crook, Dick Tain (Leonard Lord), manages to save the millionaire's daughter (Rita Coakley's Barbara Quale) from marrying the useless society youth, Owsley's Horace Winfield.

The next vehicle of the season was Harry Delf's *The Family Upstairs*, a three act comedy about a quibbling family and their eldest daughter (Rita Coakley's Louise Heller) who has a potential fiancé (Leonard Lord's Charles Grant). Owsley played the young brother, Willie. Willie was a teenager who neither worked nor attended school, and he certainly did little to win over the affections of his sister's suitor. Regardless of the various strifes, the play ends with a happily ever after for the couple.

Silence, a three act play by Max Marcin, took a turn from the over-the-top comedies of the previous weeks. The melodrama follows Jim Warren (Frank Camp), who is about to be executed for a murder he didn't commit. Owsley played Mallory, the prison's warden.

It's vague as to what Owsley did for the next production, George M. Cohan's successful four scene comedy, *The Song and Dance Man.* But the play after that was a familiar one to Owsley —David Belasco's *Kiki.* He played the stage manager, Joly. It's quite possible that this had also been his role from last summer's performance of *Kiki* from Stuart Walker.

At the end of May, the Poli Players presented *Irene,* a two act musical comedy. *Irene* was adapted from James Montgomery's book. Lyrics were written by Joseph McCarthy, and the score was done by Harry Tierney.

The musical's titular character, played by Eve Nansen, is a poor shop girl who poses as a society girl at the request of a wealthy businessman, Donald Marshall (Foster Williams). Owsley played Robert Harrison and received praise for demonstrating his musical chops. As *The Springfield Daily Republican* noted[3], he and the other male leads "literally danced and skipped about until they had no legs to stand on and no breath to go on."

J.C. and Elliott Nugent's three act college comedy, *The Poor Nut,* marked the start of June for the Poli Players. Owsley's Wallie Pierce was a friend to the complicated lead, John Miller (Foster Williams). Hesitant John transforms into a college hero after "the gentle administrations of love and psychology."[4]

The Cinderella-esque four act play *Dear Me* by Luther Reed

and Hale Hamilton was the next presentation. Eve Nansen played the role of a poor maid, April Blair, in a home for artistic and literary failures. She finds herself in New York and quickly in the spotlight thanks to her secret Prince Charming, Edgar Craig (Foster Williams). Owsley had the role of Dudley Quail, a questionable man with money who wishes to invest in April's show and eventually is instrumental in revealing Edgar's true identity.

George Abbott and John V. A. Weaver's *Love 'Em and Leave 'Em* is another play that was still enjoying a run on Broadway when Poli secured the rights to present it early. The three act play follows two sisters—Eve Nansen as the older, more responsible Mame Walsh and Elizabeth Duray as the younger, playful Janie Walsh—employed by a department store that's to hold a pageant. When Janie gambles away the pageant's funds, it's up to Mame to fix things. The role of Jim Somers allowed Owsley to demonstrate his dependable comedic gifts again as he played one of the performers who is to put on an act during the pageant.

Irish comedienne Gracie Emmett joined the Poli Players at the end of June for an elaborate vaudeville sketch she wrote herself, *Mrs. Murphy in Society*. The titular character is an Irish washwoman who suddenly becomes wealthy. Emmett had been playing the role of Mrs. Murphy since *Mrs. Murphy in Society*'s first performance in Boston in 1900.

The Poli Players were in the background for most of that week, but they had chances to shine. Owsley, as Billy Coyle, even obliged the audiences with a ballad.

The Gorilla, a three act play by Ralph Spence, was the next production from the summer stock. The mystery parody is a play within a play, and it leans more toward entertainment than plausibility. When Alice Denby (Eve Nansen) visits her uncle Walter (Cyrus Stevens), she brings along Arthur Marsden (Foster Williams). Arthur has written a mystery play, and elements of that play begin to emerge in Cyrus's life. Owsley had the role of Simmons, a reporter for the local newspaper.

Owsley was scheduled to go on vacation after *The Gorilla*. He and his father decided to watch the opening night for the next week's presentation, *Molly Darling*. It was a good thing he had stuck around because the new juvenile actor, Harry Moore, had an outburst while on stage. Moore left Frank Camp and Elizabeth Duray to do the best they could with carrying on the show while he exited the stage.

The crew turned to Owsley for help, and he readily agreed to jump in. He read Moore's part directly from the manuscript and rescued the Poli Players from a disastrous opening night. The following morning's news reported the audience "had a good time watching him go through as if it were an early rehearsal."[5]

The heroic episode would be the last mention of Owsley in the Poli Players' summer stock season for 1926. Two weeks later, Owsley's name would be seen again in the news, this time attached to the Chicago production of Owen Davis's *The Great Gatsby*, adapted from the book by F. Scott Fitzgerald.

The Great Gatsby was published in 1925 and quickly seized for the stage as a three act drama by producer William A. Brady. It had a successful, but fairly short run on Broadway at the Ambassador Theatre earlier in 1926. The Chicago production retained much of the original cast, including James Rennie, who played Jay Gatsby. Owsley was to fill in as Nick Carraway.

In the novel, Carraway is the narrator, and all characters in the story are seen through his lens. For the stage adaptation, Davis removed Carraway from the narration. Carraway's overall role is reduced to Gatsby's friend and neighbor. Many of Carraway's descriptions and insights were rewritten into lines for Gatsby.[6]

Still, it was quite a meaty part and a great opportunity for Owsley. *The Great Gatsby* opened in Chicago on August 1 at the Studebaker Theater and played for three months to enthusiastic audiences—twice longer than Brady had initially planned. Throughout October, the show was presented in different parts of New York and New Jersey.

Owsley returned to Hartford to visit his parents afterward and took a long break from acting.

1927 was a slower year for Owsley in terms of the stage. He might have dabbled in journalism, driving cars, or stage coaching instead of performing. The only play he is known to have been in for the whole year is Roland Oliver's *Night Hawk* in Philadelphia.

Night Hawk, a three act play, had William Courtenay as Dr. Colt, a surgeon who helps a worn out sex worker. Maisie Buck (Isabelle Lowe) regains her "rejuvenation" through the Steinach operation, a procedure that would allegedly fight aging, and falls for Dr. Colt's brother. Owsley played the brother, Walter. The romance is ended, though, when Dr. Colt exposes Maisie's background to Walter.

Around Halloween that year, Owsley humorously made the Long Island society papers by winning second place in the men's contest at a masquerade party. He won an "unusual" walking stick, and then he set off for a big project—filming a silent picture in Trenton, Ontario.

World War I picture *Carry On, Sergeant!* was filmed from late 1927 until May 1928. It follows a group of men who join the Canadian-Scottish regiment after the United Kingdom declared war on Germany. As a soldier and eventual acquaintance to lead Bob MacKay (Hugh Buckler), Owsley had a fair amount of screen time. His part as Leonard Sinclair, however, would go unseen by the masses.

Owsley and Hugh Buckler in Carry On, Sergeant! *(courtesy of Library and Archives Canada)*

The war drama generated much controversy upon its November 1928 release. Most of it was due to the married Sergeant MacKay's affair with another woman, but the picture also had other issues going on. The Canadian government had wanted to get into making films to rival America's projects. They didn't know what they were doing, though, so they hired "experts" that were pretty much only good at fleecing money from investors.[7]

The same experts brought a cartoonist from England into the project—Bruce Bairnsfather. Though he had been a soldier during World War I and had written a book based on his service, he notably had no experience in the picture business. Still, he wrote, directed, and produced the film. Production took nearly a year, with filming being at least seven months long. The picture cost $500,000 to make, which was a huge amount for a film in those days.

Dozens of investors and the Ontario government panicked when they saw the finished product. Aside from the controversial affair, the film also suffered from horrendous pacing, and the overall story was lacking. There were also complaints that the movie had done little to make it clear that it was a Canadian film. When the Americans show up, the Stars and Stripes flag is prominently seen, and the scenes in Paris are constructed to give a French feel (complete with the French waiter having an accent in the intertitles), but there wasn't much patriotism present for Canada outside of the credits.

Carry On, Sergeant! had a limited run in Canada, and it never had a proper release in the United States. Most of the prints of the full film were destroyed, but at least one copy was saved. The movie can now be viewed online, thanks to Library and Archives Canada.

Brenda Bond and Owsley greeting Lewis Dayton in Carry On, Sergeant! *(courtesy of Library and Archives Canada)*

Owsley didn't receive fame from the movie, and his living conditions were poor. He paid four dollars a week for room and board in Trenton during a "bitterly cold" winter. The time spent on *Carry On, Sergeant!* must have felt like a waste, but Owsley maintained some good humor about the situation.

"There was plenty of 'you-know-what' and we had a great time," he remarked to Harry N. Blair in *The New Movie*

Magazine,[8] who noted Owsley had said those words with a slow smile. Given that Ontario had officially repealed its Prohibition ordinance in 1927, "you-know-what" probably referred to alcohol, but it could have just as easily included other substances or physical pleasures.

Carry On, Sergeant! finished shooting in early May, which gave Owsley enough time to head to St. Michaels, Maryland for his next film. He had landed a role in Paramount's *The First Kiss.* The Chesapeake Bay wasn't too far from Trenton, and the climate was certainly much warmer.

Filming for *The First Kiss* started at the end of May and lasted for five weeks. Fay Wray played Anna Lee, a society girl, and Gary Cooper played Mulligan Talbot, a poor fisherman who turns to pirating in order to be wealthy enough to marry Anna. It released in August 1928 and generated fairly positive reviews. As it hit theaters before *Carry On, Sergeant!,* it's widely considered to be Owsley's first movie.

Still from The First Kiss. *The well-dressed gentleman behind the dock is the Other Suitor, Owsley. (courtesy Maryland Room at Talbot County Library)*

The First Kiss is thought to be a lost film, and hardly anything is known about Owsley's part. Reviews often focused on Wray and Cooper. When other characters were discussed, the focus extended to the Talbot family. Even the official press sheet from Paramount merely names Owsley as "Other Suitor." The full story synopsis included in the press sheet fails to reference his character.

Still, he was important enough to get his name in the credits and in multiple newspapers across the nation.

When Owsley returned to New York, he received a part on stage in Eugene O'Neill's *Strange Interlude,* replacing Earle Larrimore as Sam. However, he found himself too fatigued to actually play the role. Owsley came to an agreement with the Theater Guild, quit the show, and spent his summer playing tennis at Forest Hills.

"Everybody was awfully mad at me," Owsley later told Winifred Aydelotte in an interview.[9] "They said I was giving up the biggest opportunity ever offered [to] me. And I was. But it all worked out for the best."

That was true. The turning point in Owsley's career came later that fall.

And it might have been a flat tire that changed the course of his life.

CHAPTER THREE

The Film Daily[1] reported that Monroe Owsley had been traveling from Long Island to see a producer about a part in a Broadway production. His tire "went blooey," prompting him to lose the part in the show. But the very next day, he was offered a part in a different show—Philip Barry's three act comedy, *Holiday*.

Holiday showed early previews under the name *The Dollar* a week before it premiered at the Plymouth (currently known as the Gerald Schoenfeld Theatre) on November 26, 1928. It follows a wealthy family whose values are scrutinized when the younger daughter, Julia Seton (Dorothy Tree), brings home a fiancé. Johnny Case (Ben Smith) has little interest in working and making money. Friction divides the family as the older daughter, Linda Seton (Hope Williams), sees her reflection in Johnny and falls in love with him.

Owsley played the blasé brother, Ned Seton, who drinks excessively to cope with the stifled life his family's wealth and place in society has brought him. Ned at first appears to serve as comic relief, making his grand entrance while looking for a missing cocktail shaker. But his contempt for the snobbish Julia and their equally self-centered father (Walter Walker) is instantly established, and he soon proves himself to be Linda's most trusted confidant.

There is a palpable ache that emerges toward the end when Linda offers to take Ned away with her—away from the family and high society—and his hopes are immediately dashed by their father and his own internalized fears. Linda promises to come back for her brother, and he responds (almost inaudibly, as the script calls for) that he'll "be here."[2]

Still, the play closes with Ned proposing a toast to Linda after she goes against her father and leaves to find Johnny, who has broken his engagement to Julia. There is hope that Ned might chase his own happy ending one day, just as Linda has chosen to do.

Owsley received much praise from crowds and critics alike for this role. Even reviews that had criticism for the script or the other actors almost always had something kind to say about Owsley. Arthur Pollock insinuated in his column that Owsley had more stage experience than most of the cast, which might have given his performance more of a polished finish than the rest.[3]

All of the attention caught Owsley off-guard, as he recalled in *The New Movie Magazine.* "I'd played more important parts on the road without causing a ripple."[4]

Holiday ran for an impressive two hundred and twenty-nine performances. Whatever issues there might have been from critics, audiences continued showing up for performances. The cast and their acting had won over the hearts of theater-goers.

As a notable aside, *Holiday* had a new actress, Katharine Hepburn, as the understudy for Williams. Hepburn would later go on to play the part of Linda in the 1938 film version of the play.

When *Holiday* closed in June of 1929, Owsley took a break. The summer went by with little activity from him worth making it to the news. He checked in at Forest Hills in September with his father for a few weeks, and then he left to rejoin the *Holiday* company for a road version of the production.

The play reopened at the Plymouth toward the end of October with its original cast. All through November, the cast performed in Newark, Brooklyn, and Philadelphia.

Early on in 1930, theater producer Henry Duff wanted to stage a Los Angeles production of *Holiday*. Naturally, Owsley leaped at the chance to reprise his role in a new environment. He wired an acceptance and drove across the country with his friend and fellow actor, Warren Ashe. Ashe also had a theatrical engagement on the West Coast to fulfill. The pair stopped in El Paso to visit with Owsley's brother and sister-in-law during their journey.

When Owsley and Ashe arrived in California, Owsley learned that Duff had decided to postpone the Los Angeles production. It's possible Owsley might have been given a role in the play that replaced *Holiday* at the Hollywood Playhouse, Ida Lublenski's *Helena's Boys*. This is unconfirmed, though.

By the time Duff was ready to put on *Holiday* in April, Owsley was already involved in a different project—production for the screen version of *Holiday* had started.

Pathé Studios hired Edward H. Griffith to direct, and Horace Jackson adapted *Holiday* for the screen. It was a sensible choice to ask Owsley to reprise his role for the film, but it didn't hurt that he shared some "cameo-type of features"[5] with the film's leading women, Ann Harding and Mary Astor.

Owsley spent the late spring shooting, and he was possibly thrilled about being reunited with his old pal, Harding. He also had another person from the stage production on the set with him, Elizabeth Forrester. Forrester had played a maid on the stage, and now she had a larger role as Laura Cram.

Holiday was a smashing success when it premiered in the summer of 1930. The film version retained much of Barry's witty, yet acidic dialogue, and it's easy to see how Owsley shined on the stage as Ned Seton.

Though the movie eases into Ned's drinking, his world-weary viewpoint is immediately apparent. One of Ned's first lines has him snappily remark "we don't need a saint in this family" while the Seton daughters (Harding as Linda and Astor as Julia) discuss Johnny (Robert Ames)'s background.

The handsome, well-dressed son transforms into a sloppy, drunken mess during the party announcing Julia and Johnny's engagement. Ned defends his drinking to Julia while quibbling with her. "It's my protection against your friends," he says bluntly. Ned is every bit the decent brother that Linda deserves while he comforts her.

Ann Harding and Owsley in Holiday. *Ned's on the verge of passing out, but he's still there for his sister. (from author's personal collection)*

When Ned delivers his last toast, though he is resentful of his situation, the hope in his face is visibly bright.

Though the film is visually pleasing and well edited, it has its share of technical issues. Being a product of the early talkies, the sound recording equipment had its limitations. The camera can be heard in many scenes, and the sound cuts out completely at times. The dialogue doesn't flow naturally, either, since no one could overlap each other. Astor expressed her frustrations about it in her memoir.[6]

"You couldn't talk and pace up and down. For example, if the action started with you standing beside a table and then included a move to a chair by the fireplace, you could speak into a mike at the table, but you couldn't talk on the way over; you'd have to wait until you sat down—where there was another mike in the fireplace!"

Limitations aside, *Holiday* did tremendously well. This success changed the trajectory of Monroe Owsley's career. His stage days were now over. The film world seemed so full of possibilities for the ambitious actor.

Unfortunately, Owsley's career wouldn't go quite the way he wanted it to go. His dissatisfaction with the world of movies would emerge again and again.

During a 1931 *Silver Screen* interview with S.R. Mook, Owsley complained about how the ending of *Holiday* had changed.[7]

"In 'Holiday'—on the stage—instead of ending where Linda rushes out the door to the taxi, it ends with the old man telling Ned to go to the pier and stop the boat. When Ned refuses, he says, 'I'll go myself.' Ned laughs at him, locks the door and cuts the telephone wires, grabs a glass and says 'To Linda.'"

"It was a grand finish because it shows that Ned wasn't basically a weakling and that he was capable of doing something as big for his sister as she had tried to do for him. But *that* scene was cut out pretty quick in the picture, I can tell you."

However, there's currently little evidence the stage or film production ever had such an ending. It's possible this story was an invention of Owsley's imagination during his nervous breakdown—which will be covered later in this book.

Marquis Busby wrote an article on Owsley around the same

time where Owsley, perhaps a bit paradoxically, insisted that Ned wasn't weak at all. "He just showed good sense by staying drunk in that family."[8]

Owsley's next project after *Holiday* was another production for Pathé. *Kid the Kidder* was a comedy short, two reels long, written by Paul Dickey and directed by Ray McCarey. In the short, college seniors decide to trick a new student into going on a date with a "widow" (Vera Marsh). A fictitious husband threateningly appears during the date, and the freshman, realizing what's going on, gets the police and an ambulance to help him exact revenge on the seniors.

Promotional graphic for Kid the Kidder. *(courtesy Everett Collection)*

It's most likely Owsley played one of the seniors hazing the freshman. *Kid the Kidder* was quickly shot in September and released not too long after. The short is presumably lost now.

The fall proved to be a busy season for Owsley. He was cast in a picture for Universal Studios and a film for Columbia Pictures around the same time. While shooting those movies, he was cast in a film for Paramount Pictures. This was when an article emerged about Owsley's father offering him five thousand dollars to finish his schedule in time to be home for Christmas. Owsley easily won the bet, finishing his Universal and Columbia obligations in November and returning to the East Coast for the holidays. The Paramount production would film in their New York studio.

The *Los Angeles Times* reported in November that Paramount had decided to sign a long-term contract with Owsley.[9] This was the studio era of Hollywood—stars were made and controlled by big studios, like Fox (later, Twentieth Century-Fox), Metro-Goldwyn-Mayer (MGM), Paramount, RKO, and Warner Brothers. The contract would have offered Owsley stable income and steady work in exchange for him acting exclusively with them.

However, shortly after the winter holidays were over, Owsley went back to Hollywood to work on a picture for United Artists. The contract with Paramount had either been broken or was never inked in the first place.

Universal's *Free Love,* directed by Hobart Henley, released in December of 1930. The (apparently comedic) romance was adapted from a play by Sidney Howard, *Half Gods.* Genevieve Tobin starred as Hope Ferrier, who is unhappy in her marriage to Stephen Ferrier, played by Conrad Nagel. It earned mixed reviews from film critics.

In *Free Love,* Hope decides to leave her husband. Rush Bigelow, played by Owsley, is Stephen's best friend with "a weakness for pretty women."[10] Rush and Hope go together to Atlantic City, seeking quality time away from Stephen. This trips earns Rush a punch in the jaw from Stephen. The estranged couple end up reconciling, despite Stephen also hitting Hope right in the jaw, leaving Rush in the dust.

Rightfully, a few critics questioned the choice of domestic abuse creating a happily ever after for the couple. Still, *Free Love* interrogated the institution of monogamy, reflecting the questions on the minds of that generation's free-spirited young adults.

Conrad Nagel delivering a punch to Owsley while Genevieve Tobin watches in Free Love. *This would be the first of many times Owsley gets clobbered on screen. (courtesy Everett Collection)*

During the same month as *Free Love*'s release, Owsley demonstrated that he still had an interest in writing. An opinion column penned by him appeared in *The Film Daily*.[11]

Hollywood Stimulates American Sightseeing

The film industry, centralized in Hollywood, has done more to stimulate the "See America First," movement than any other one factor. The eastern people had not paid much attention to the appeal of "See America First" until Hollywood began to spread its fame to the four corners of the globe, but today they are seeing their own country,

> *incidental to the trip to Hollywood and the Pacific Coast. The patriotic appeal had little effect in stemming the tide of European travel by Americans, but when America began an attraction that had no rival in any other country, then she began to enjoy the tourist trade of her own citizens. That attraction is Hollywood. In coming to Hollywood, travelers have discovered the other wonders of the West that have been talked about for years, but toward which no attention could be aroused. They have taken back their accounts of these wonders and now have started a great volume of travel to the West of which Hollywood is no longer the sole objective. But I think the film capital should have much of the credit for starting it. —Monroe Owsley*

The See America First campaign had started early in the twentieth century at a time when wealthy East Coasters were spending a fortune vacationing in Europe instead of America. As railroad systems expanded and automobiles appeared, tourism within America increased exponentially. This coincided with the rise of Hollywood, so Owsley wasn't entirely off the mark in his observations.

Columbia Pictures's *Ten Cents a Dance* released in January of 1931. The film's title and story was inspired by a popular song of the same name. The dramatic romance follows a taxi dancer named Barbara O'Neill (Barbara Stanwyck), who falls in marries the wrong man and gets rescued by her customer who's in love with her. Ricardo Cortez played the wealthy dance hall patron, Bradley Carlton, and Owsley played Barbara's husband, Eddie Miller.

From the film's onset, the audience can see kind-hearted Bradley is the one for Barbara, but Eddie initially proves to be gentle, despite needing to borrow money from her. His true colors begin to show when he discovers her profession—he makes a scene at the dance hall, gets into a fight, and embarrasses her publicly over a fit of jealousy. Still, Barbara winds up marrying Eddie.

Owsley, Barbara Stanwyck, and Pat Harmon after a scuffle in Ten Cents a Dance. *(courtesy Everett Collection)*

It's not long after marriage that Eddie starts criticizing Barbara's housekeeping, gambling, cheating on his wife, and stealing money from Bradley. He even blames his crimes on Barbara instead of himself. When Barbara rescues Eddie from debt by borrowing money from Bradley, Eddies accuses her of infidelity instead of showing an ounce of gratitude or guilt.

Barbara stands up for herself after Eddie delivers the biggest insult—giving her a dime for a dance. She wakes up to her situation and calls Eddie out on his cowardice and scumminess. Stanwyck's finest performance in the movie is during this argument where she tells Eddie she doesn't love him. "You're not a man. You're not even a good sample," she says mournfully.

The movie ends with Bradley proposing to Barbara—a trip to Paris, where she could obtain a divorce, and then be free to marry him. Eddie manages to escape with no legal repercussions or even another physical fight. All that's been hurt is his ego.

Ten Cents a Dance reunited Owsley with Lionel Barrymore, who was the film's director. It would ultimately be Barrymore's last movie he directed. His health had declined due to arthritis, and pain management made it difficult to carry out his duties behind the camera. According to Cortez, there wasn't much direction during the process. Barrymore would fall asleep while in the director's chair due to his medication.

Despite this, the cast had respect for Barrymore and sympathized with his situation. They gave it their all to make the film, even at the expense of their health. Notably, Stanwyck took a serious fall, but she returned to the set as soon as possible. "Backing away from Monroe Owsley, in my desire to be vehement—overacting, I think people would call it—I fell down the stairs," she said. Her performance on screen doesn't show any sign of an injury.[12]

Owsley would continue to lavish praise for Barrymore in the years to come, referring to him in an interview with *The Knoxville Journal* as a "good sport."[13]

Ten Cents a Dance showed strong potential with its great cast, but the lack of direction is noticeable. Contemporaneous reviews of the film often noted its pacing issues and weak story. Praise, however, was always given to Stanwyck, Owsley, and Cortez. Owsley played the villainous, narcissistic husband to perfection.

Honor Among Lovers was released by Paramount in February. Claudette Colbert played Julia Traynor, a personal secretary to Wall Street trader Jerry Stafford (Frederic March). Jerry is happy as a carefree single man, but he also loves Julia immensely. Julia, who wants a husband and stability, can't bring herself to commit to a yearlong trip as Jerry's lover. Instead, she chooses a future with a struggling trader, Philip Craig.

After getting married (and subsequently fired by Jerry), Julia discovers her husband is a terrible man. This man, of course, is played by our dear Monroe Owsley.

Just like in *Ten Cents a Dance,* Owsley's character quickly proves himself to be all wrong for the heroine. Philip embezzles funds, gets obnoxiously drunk in public after he loses the stolen money, and accuses his wife of selling herself to Jerry when she receives a bailout from her former boss. He even manages to shoot Jerry in a moment of desperation. Owsley embodies the scoundrel character as Philip tries to blame the shooting on Julia while also begging her to help him.

Owsley, Claudette Colbert, and Frederic March at the end of Honor Among Lovers. *(courtesy Everett Collection)*

Jerry's a nice guy who is still in love with Julia, though, and he refuses to pursue further legal actions against Philip after having the shooting ruled as an accident. Julia leaves her husband despite his protests, and the movie ends with Julia and Jerry talking about a trip to France.

Owsley might have turned down the opportunity to work in *Honor Among Lovers,* but he was quite drawn to the director, Dorothy Arzner. In *The New Movie Magazine,* Owsley "confesses" that he had only ever written two fan letters, and one was to Arzner.

("The other concerns a story which is too long to tell here," Blair teases readers.)

Arzner was famous in Hollywood for her strong feminist gaze in the movies she directed. The protagonists were often women who didn't conform neatly to society's conservative expectations, especially in regards to romance and sex. Arzner herself didn't conform to society's expectations at the time. She frequently wore suits, and it was an open secret that she was a lesbian. Even getting to the position of director required her to challenge the male-dominated industry's idea of who could make a movie.

Honor Among Lovers's ending reflects an enduring theme of Arzner's works where women choose their own happiness. Julia's disastrous marriage upends her conception of what matrimony and stability really mean. She chooses to leave Philip, but she doesn't immediately plan to marry Jerry. For the time being, a trip as someone's lover is enough.

Reviews of *Honor Among Lovers* at the time often compared it with *Ten Cents a Dance.* Despite the films being released by two different studios, it's hard not to make comparisons with the similar stories and Owsley portraying the same type of caddish character. The near simultaneous release also didn't help. Of the two movies, though, *Honor Among Lovers* is the stronger film—the pacing is better, there are more scenes between the heroine and the "right one," and Owsley's descent into villainy isn't quite as cartoonish.

In May, Owsley's next film, *Indiscreet,* was released by United

Artists. Gloria Swanson starred as the heroine, Jerry Trent, trying to protect her sister Joan (Barbara Kent) from her dastardly ex-lover.

As one might have guessed already, Owsley played said ex-lover, Jim Woodward. His sneer is topped with a tacky mustache to help establish his inherent sleaziness.

Director Leo McCarey had a gift for comedies, and *Indiscreet* opens with plenty of laughs. Jerry breaks up with Jim coolly after he cheats on her one too many times. "A man must live," he defends himself. "I've often wondered why it was necessary in some cases," she retorts.

When Jim proposes to Jerry in a moment of desperation, she laughs ever so sweetly, but the bitterness can be heard in every ripple. As Jim leaves her apartment, Jerry teases him with a bit false hope, asking him to come back—then she gives him his golf clubs.

Jerry soon falls into a romance with an author, Tony Blake (Ben Lyon), who proposes marriage at their first meeting. As their relationship progresses, Jerry confesses that she isn't a virgin in a subtle 1930s way, and Tony asks her to promise to never see that man again. She promises.

Then, her younger sister returns from Paris, gushing about a man she met. Unease shrouds Jerry when Joan says Jim Woodward's name. A series of shenanigans unfolds as Jerry attempts to separate Joan and Jim. This plan ends with Jerry luring Jim into seducing her where Joan can catch them—inadvertently, so does Tony.

Everything works out for Jerry and Tony in the end, though, down to them asking a ship captain to marry them so they can share a cabin.

Owsley and Gloria Swanson breaking up in Indiscreet. *(courtesy Everett Collection)*

Indiscreet received fairly positive reviews, despite its frail plot. It was very much a vehicle for Swanson. She sang two songs with her charming voice and was every bit as stunning as she had been in her silent films. Everyone else in the cast, even Owsley, seem dull in comparison to her shine.

Owsley enjoyed his time on the set, as he told Busby. "I loved working with Gloria Swanson. She is amazingly generous with the people in her cast. It was a lot of fun."[14]

The cast of *Indiscreet* had an interesting recreational activity while shooting the picture. Lyon had received a license to pilot a plane for his role as an aviator in 1930's *Hell's Angels,* and he regularly relaxed after a day's shooting by flying. Arthur Lake—who played Buster Collins in *Indiscreet*—also had flying experience due to 1928's *The Air Circus,* and he asked to ride along. Soon, the rest of the cast received rides from Lyon. Owsley, who initially had been hesitant, became a devout air enthusiast.

Swanson surprised everybody one evening by flying onto the field with a plane she had chartered. She then challenged Lyon and Owsley to a race. Who won? Articles didn't report the result, but everyone appeared to have a good time.[15]

The rapid release of *Free Love, Ten Cents a Dance, Honor Among Lovers,* and *Indiscreet* within months of each other cemented the direction of Owsley's film career. *Photoplay*[16] referred to Owsley as the "Ace of Cads" in their review of *Honor Among Lovers,* an apt sobriquet for an actor who played weaselly roles tremendously well. This type of character would be permanently associated with Owsley. His sulky sneer became his signature, and his characters' inevitable betrayals were foreshadowed by his presence alone.

As with many actors who experience typecasting, Owsley detested it. Even in his stock theater days, he had expressed frustration about always having a comedic role and not a romantic one. Owsley managed to stop being typecasted in comedic roles by 1931, but he now had a new character that he hated even more.

It didn't help that the role that was to transform him into a romantic lead was publicly taken away from him.

CHAPTER FOUR

In February of 1931, Monroe Owsley signed with MGM for a movie directed by Clarence Brown as one of the male leads. Norma Shearer was the female lead, and Clark Gable was the other male lead. But Owsley was dropped for some reason and replaced by Leslie Howard in *A Free Soul.*

Interestingly, later in the year, Owsley signed for another movie, *Sporting Blood,* with Clark Gable at MGM. He also was eventually dropped that production.

Two major news articles came out in March pertaining to Owsley. First, he had been signed for a long term contract with MGM. Second, he had been cast as Joan Crawford's leading man in *Girls Together,* a movie adapted from Mildred Cram's story of the same title.

Owsley and Crawford may have had some kind of romantic past. During promotions for *Girls Together, Motion Picture Magazine* reported "Monroe and Joan, in early Broadway days, were once Like That about each other and that Joan promised to wait for him to make his fortune."[1] However, about a year later, *Photoplay* ran an article recounting a time in 1928 when Owsley had had tea with columnist Katherine Albert. While they chatted, he confessed he had adored Crawford, but she had never loved him. Albert wrote "he may now say he and Joan were sweethearts, but she never held out false hopes to him."[2]

Crawford doesn't mention Owsley in her memoirs, nor do most of her biographers bring him up except in a professional capacity. Whatever their relationship had actually been, it's fair to assume they at least enjoyed each other's company while filming.

Owsley and Joan Crawford in Photoplay *during* Girls Together *publicity. Crawford and Douglas Fairbanks, Jr. were THE Hollywood couple at the time. (courtesy Media History Digital Library)*

Owsley, Crawford, and professional tennis player Harvey Snodgrass posing together at the tennis court. (courtesy Stephanie Jones at www.joancrawfordbest.com)

Owsley and Crawford were both tennis enthusiasts, and they often raced to the courts after leaving the studio. Owsley had taken lessons some time back from William Tilden. Tilden was considered one of the greatest tennis players before his multiple arrests for soliciting sex from underage boys in the 1940s caused his downfall.

While they shot the film, publicity photos of Owsley and Crawford playing tennis appeared in newspapers. The press detailed Owsley's drunken and caddish ways in his film career thus far, and they all anticipated his screen reformation as a romantic lead.

Owsley himself voiced his desire for a change in his image during these promotions. He expressed his opinion that if there were no prohibition law, the demand for the alcohol revelers would go down.

George Shaffer reported that Owsley had said his ambition wasn't to make a million dollars, but "merely to play one good part where I don't have to be continuously inebriated on the screen."[3]

"I can play weaklings and villains when I'm 40. Right at the present I want to get the heroine in the final clinch," Owsley told Marquis Busby in a different interview.[4]

"I tried very hard to escape that type of role after 'Holiday.' I went into 'Ten Cents a Dance' in the belief that it was a story about redemption, and in the same way I was fooled on 'Honor Among Lovers.' 'Indiscreet' isn't so bad, for me. It has a lot of humor."

Busby's article ended on a positive note that Owsley would get to marry Crawford in *Girls Together.*

Early previews for *Girls Together,* now titled *This Modern Age, did* show an ending where Owsley marries Crawford. *Motion Picture Herald*'s review in their June 13 issue delivered a sufficient synopsis of the movie's story.[5]

Crawford played Valentine "Val" Winters, a young adult who reunites with her mother (Marjorie Rambeau) in Paris after a lifetime apart. Val's mother is a mistress to a French man (played by Armand Kaliz), and she's friends with a rambunctious crowd with liberal ideas of love and alcohol. One of those friends include Owsley's Tony Girard, an American who is happily enjoying all of life's pleasures in Paris.

Val and Tony become infatuated with each other, but Val's affections waver when she meets Bob Blake (Neil Hamilton) after a car accident caused by a loaded Tony. Bob is from a conservative family, and Val gives up her party lifestyle in order to marry him. Everything then falls apart when his parents meet her mother and their merrymaking friends.

With the engagement broken, Val travels to Normandy with Tony. When Tony realizes Val is "giving herself to him" without love in her heart, he decides to leave. At this point, Val sees Tony's sincerity, which awakens her buried love for him. Val's mother arrives at the end to witness Val and Tony getting married.

Marjorie Rambeau watching Owsley and Crawford hug each other in the first version of This Modern Age. *(courtesy Stephanie Jones at www.joancrawfordbest.com)*

Studio executives at MGM saw this version, and they weren't pleased with it (and, according to Florabel Muir, Crawford also disliked it)[6]. The studio spent around $200,000 to remake the film. Nick Grinde, the director, was reportedly replaced by Clarence Brown for the reshoots.[7] Several of the cast members were also replaced, including Rambeau and Kaliz. Pauline Frederick took over the role of Val's mother, Diane, and Albert Conti played André de Graignon, Diane's lover. Much of the script was rewritten.

The biggest change was Val would end up with Bob instead of Tony. Owsley went from being the romantic lead to the film's comic relief. The understandably frustrated actor vented to anyone who would listen.

"I'm tired of being the society play-boy with a glass in my hand," Owsley complained to Harrison Carroll.[8]

Owsley's contract with MGM was mutually dissolved after the reshoots.

In late August, the final version of *This Modern Age* hit theaters. The movie's story received mixed reviews, but the visuals were well-received. *This Modern Age* gave the world a rare look at a blonde Crawford—her hair had been dyed to match Rambeau's flaxen locks, and there hadn't been much need to change it during reshoots with Frederick. Legendary costume designer Adrian provided gorgeous, sleek silk gowns for Crawford. The film's various backdrops are also quite striking. MGM had built an extravagant set with a swimming pool inside a fancy restaurant, and Crawford shows off her splendid figure before diving into the water.

This Modern Age used new technology to film its dancing scenes, helping the busy moments feel more natural.[9] The dancing microphone was lighter than the standard cylindrical dialogue microphone, allowing it be held above Owsley and Crawford's tango sequence in a large ballroom. Compared to *Indiscreet,* where Owsley and Swanson's dancing scene has choppy quality and limited dialogue, the sound and flow of conversation in *This Modern Age* is vastly better.

Though the rewritten script hadn't done much to make a stronger story and the film ends rather abruptly, the movie is overall enjoyable. Regardless of who is Val's true love interest, the heart of the story rests in her relationship with her mother. When Diane abandons her daughter in a misguided attempt to make Val more acceptable to Bob's family, Val's grief can be felt through the screen. Joy only returns to her face when she reunites with her mother in the film's last few seconds.

For all the contempt he must have felt, Owsley still gave it his all in *This Modern Age.* Owsley is quite the scene stealer with his character's various shenanigans, and his performance didn't go unnoticed by audiences. Even the film's staunchest critics had good words for Owsley.

Owsley embracing Joan Crawford in This Modern Age. *(courtesy Everett Collection)*

All of the movie's outlandish moments hinge on Tony's party habits and resistance to marriage. He dives into the restaurant's swimming pool while in a tux without thinking twice about it. "I love you too much to put you in jail for life," he quips to Val during one party scene. The next morning, he is found sleeping under Diane's bear, scaring the household staff while snoozing. The car accident he causes while drinking and driving is so silly, it almost makes sense no one gets hurt. While Bob escorts Val and Tony home from the accident, Tony stops for a nap on a bench.

Despite his reluctance to commitment, Tony's affections for

Val stay true. From the start of the movie to the end, he pursues her earnestly, but not cruelly. He only loses once Bob shoves him aside, forcibly throws Val over his shoulder, and takes her to meet her mother.

The remake of *This Modern Age* was hastily done, and communications with the marketing departments were lacking. After the film's release, there were theaters, newspapers, and fan magazines still erroneously reporting that Owsley was the picture's romantic interest. Rambeau and Kaliz were also mentioned in some promotion material, despite them not being in the final product.

For all the praise Owsley received in *This Modern Age*, his tenure with MGM certainly had a negative impact on him. He took a vacation to San Francisco around the movie's release. When he came back, he sold his Beverly Hills home and moved into an apartment, claiming a house felt empty without a woman.

By October, he was in the Glendale Sanitarium.[10]

The official cause given was that Owsley had suffered a nervous breakdown. It's safe to assume the fiasco at MGM had contributed to his poor mental health. While there might have been other issues at play, such as his mother's own extended stay in a sanitarium, Owsley's frustrations with his career and image had clearly reached his limit. An interview with S.R. Mook that ran in *Silver Screen* magazine coincidentally during the same time he checked into the sanitarium reveals a lot.[11]

Though Mook tried to get Owsley to see the silver lining of his film career, he didn't back down from his stance. The interview took place after a double holiday where Owsley had been in "sleepless worry" over what to do with his career.

"They're not going to 'type' me," he said. "I'll go back to the stage first, and do the things I know I can do, even if it means giving up my contract."

He brought up *This Modern Age* during the interview as well.

"I was all puffed up about the part in 'This Modern Age' and gave it all I had. It was something different. I got the girl in the end. Now, they've rewritten the whole thing and Neil Hamilton gets her. That burns me up. I never get a girl."

Owsley claimed that MGM had promised they wouldn't typecast him when he signed the long term contract with them. While protesting he could play romantic leads, he claimed he did romantic parts on the stage. This doesn't align with his known stage history, but nearly all of his academy plays are currently unknown.

The interview also reveals that Owsley had an alcohol problem.

"I tried to play and work at the same time," he told Mook. "It can't be done. Besides the late hours, it was a cocktail here and a highball there. I finally had to call 'quits.' I'm on the wagon now and I've taken a house down at the beach. The next time you come down, you'll drink lemonade and like it. Moreover, we go to bed at nine o'clock."

He continued to be quite blunt about his jaded view of Hollywood.

"It seems to me that everybody out here worries more than is good for anyone. They worry over parts, they worry over pictures, they worry over publicity and they even worry—seriously—over whether they look their best when they go out anywhere. It's beginning to hand me a big laugh."

His rant ended momentarily on a somber note. "I've reached the point where I can't worry anymore. I haven't got any nerves: they're numb."

Mook had some sympathy for the tense actor, noting that Hollywood executives were overlooking their players' mental health for their personal gain.

In November, Owsley left the sanitarium and was well enough to do screen tests. *Variety* reported that his father had gone to Hollywood to see Owsley while he was ill.[12] In

December, Owsley traveled for two weeks on the *S.S. Virginia* and arrived in New York right before Christmas.

He spent the holidays with his family, and then he returned to Hollywood in early January. His manager at the time, Wally Ross, sent a report that though he had improved, Owsley wasn't ready to return to work yet. Ross suggested the pair would take a trip to Honolulu in the near future.

The rest of the winter passed with few mentions of Owsley in the newspapers or fan magazines. *Screenland* belatedly announced in January that he (and a fellow frustrated actor, Leslie Howard) had renounced Hollywood. In February, Owsley was allegedly taking new tests for pictures, and he certainly was spotted as a spectator at polo games, which were popular with Hollywood celebrities at the time.

By May of 1932, Owsley was back on the lot for MGM and working on a picture, *Unashamed*.

More publicity began to appear for him that summer. *The New Movie Magazine* updated readers to let them know Owsley was back in Hollywood and slowly recovering from his nervous breakdown.[13] *The Atlanta Journal* included a write up about him in their special scoop detailing Georgia-born screen stars.[14] Owsley's silver and white roadster got a mention in the news since he spent much time at the Grand Hotel resort in Santa Monica.[15]

His name even appeared next to Joan Crawford's again during a series of articles journaling her rise to stardom.

During the summer before, Crawford and Owsley had been dancing at the night club inside the Ambassador Hotel, the Cocoanut Grove. A man from Kansas City tried to cut between them, but Joan refused. The Kansas man had interfered with a romance Joan had pursued back when she had been a waitress, thinking that no fraternity member of his should go with the girl known as Billie Cassin.

"'I don't recognize people who wouldn't recognize me,' she said. Monroe Owsley grinned and whirled her away."[16]

A July issue of *Motion Picture* magazine insinuated that Owsley had a romantic interest in Ethelind Terry.[17] This bit of gossip is notable because it was the first publicized hint of an actual romantic connection for Owsley in his cinema career.

Prior to his nervous breakdown, *Motion Picture* had noted that Hollywood hadn't been able to "scent out a romance" for Owsley. "One night he escorts Genevieve Tobin, the next Joan Marsh. And the third night, it's Betty Pierce."[18]

It's hard not to wonder if the homosexual rumors Lawrence J. Quirk referenced in *Fasten Your Seat Belts,* whether founded or unfounded, about Owsley's private life contributed to his nervous breakdown. The difference in gossip reports after his health hiatus are dramatically noticeable. Before his breakdown, little was printed about his private affairs. Upon his return to Hollywood, the reports became numerous, as if to prove something. The link to Ethelind Terry would only be the first of many.

In July, MGM released *Unashamed.* Owsley was officially back in pictures after nearly a year away from the screen.

The movie's villain was, of course, the Ace of Cads.

CHAPTER FIVE

Monroe Owsley played a particularly greasy villain in *Unashamed*. Notorious gambler Harry Swift targets young Joan Ogden (Helen Twelvetrees), who is the heir to three million dollars. While she falls for him instantly, Joan's family doesn't want her to be associated with him.

Harry's father (Jean Hersholt), a humble immigrant from Germany named Heinrich Schmidt, also doesn't want his son involved with Joan. Instead of high class and luxury, Heinrich wants his son to settle down and run the family grocery store with him. Harry, whose real name is August Schmidt, goes to his father for two thousand dollars in an attempt to make himself seem worthy to marry Joan. Heinrich initially resists, but Harry has him wrapped around his finger.

"Don't you love me anymore, Pop?" Harry asks. Forlorn, Heinrich replies, "Ya, that's the problem."

Tensions rise when Harry devises a plot to ensure Joan's family will force a wedding between them—he'll take her to a hotel and "ruin" her. Joan and Harry falsely register as a married couple at the hotel without either of their families knowing where they really are. Joan's sudden absence worries her overprotective younger brother, Dick (Robert Young). He wakes their father (played by Robert Warwick) and declares his intention to look for his missing sister.

The next morning, a trusting Joan dreams of the future as Harry soothes her worries. "A shotgun wedding!" she exclaims with a giggle.

Owsley and Helen Twelvetrees as star-crossed lovers (well, she's star-crossed) in Unashamed. *(courtesy Everett Collection)*

They go to her father and tell them what they've done, but Mr. Ogden still refuses to give his consent for their marriage. Dick returns from searching all night and goes to attack Harry for sleeping with Joan. Harry punches Dick, who scrambles away. In an indignant fury, Harry starts proclaiming he'll tell everyone about what he did with Joan.

Dick then returns with a handgun and shoots Harry, killing him. "Tell them that, too, tell them that!"

The rest of the movie details the ensuing trial and Joan's refusal to help her brother. Supposedly, the only defense for Dick is "the unwritten law."

The district attorney, played by John Miljan, is supposed to be the villain for the rest of the film, but he's not exactly wrong in his case. "There's no such thing as the unwritten law," he passionately proclaims. When it comes to the matter of Joan's "honor" being taken from her, he retorts that there's no evidence she was coerced into having sex with Harry.

"Her honor is her own, and the shortest word in the English language will protect any woman's honor, and that word is 'No.'"

The trial proceeds, and Dick's lawyer (Lewis Stone) tries to claim there's no proof a murder was committed—that it was just an accident. Several blunders occur (with Dick outright lying about what happened), and it soon emerges that the only way for Dick to avoid the electric chair is for Joan to aid him. Joan refuses for most of the movie, but she changes her mind when she reads about a possible execution.

After acting like a "disgraced" woman and giving up her social reputation, Joan demonstrates that being with Harry corrupted her. This is enough to win Dick an acquittal. The Ogdens are left to be a happy family again.

Columnist George Shaffer wrote a blunt take on the Hollywood industry after visiting the set of *Unashamed,* then known as *Without Shame.*[1] He referred to a highly publicized murder trial from the previous year that seemed to have inspired *Unashamed.* "If it weren't for newspaper headlines and wire service reports the movie corporations would have to spend money to buy plots which they now get ready made out of the columns on page 1."

Helven Twelvetrees biographer, Cliff Aliperti, connected *Unashamed* and another 1932 film (*Two Against the World*) to the death of Francis Donaldson III.[2] Francis had been seeing a society girl, Rose Allen. During an argument with Rose's family that turned physical, Francis was shot and killed by Rose's brother, Edward. Edward was ultimately acquitted on the grounds of self-defense.

The news sensationalized "honor" killings and "the unwritten law," which screenplay writer Bayard Veillier and director Harry Beaumont seemed to focus on for *Unashamed*. The film's exaggerations of the actual case didn't make for a stronger movie, unfortunately.

Time's review of *Unashamed* notes that "a hole in [Francis]'s side and none in his elbow indicated that he had had his arm raised to strike," which led the jury to acquit Edward on self-defense.[3] The self-defense angle isn't even considered in *Unashamed*.

Several reviews of the time remarked that it was the exceptional cast that saved *Unashamed* from its story. Twelvetrees, Young, and the rest of the cast all delivered emotional performances. Owsley's caddish role almost seems like a caricature of his past similar roles, but his appearance alone is fantastic at evoking disgust in the audience.

Near unbelievable story aside, the dynamic between Joan and Dick borders on unrealistic and even uncomfortable. Dick has a fiancée (Gertrude Michael), but he spends more time on the screen kissing and embracing his sister. *Unashamed* even ends with a clinch shot between the siblings usually reserved for romantic couples. This particular researcher thought the overwrought affection was a product of its time, but a few reviews from the era also noted the strange lip-locking. The affection is clearly intended to demonstrate the closeness between Joan and Dick, but its over-the-topness is distracting.

Unashamed did bring some innovation to the court drama thriller genre. The set was modeled after an ultra-modernistic courthouse in Alabama, and an attorney was on set to ensure every line of dialogue and action conformed to court etiquette and legal precedent.[4] Why self-defense wasn't brought up still remains a mystery.

Shortly after *Unashamed*'s release, Owsley joined the cast of Fox's *Hat Check Girl*. Around the same time, Owsley was reported to be "interested in" blues singer, Milla Sonde (who would soon go back to her real name, Lillian Miles).[5]

Hat Check Girl released in September. It starred Sally Eilers as Gerry Marsh, a hat check girl in a nightclub surrounded by rich and scummy people. Ben Lyon played millionaire playboy, Buster Collins (no relation to the *Indiscreet* character), who will ultimately make Gerry his wife. The movie's antagonist, Tod Reese, is the owner of a gossip magazine that he uses to blackmail people. Tod was played by, of course, Monroe Owsley.

Much like in *Unashamed,* Tod also gets shot and killed. In the review for *Hat Check Girl* by the *New York Times,* it's humorously noted "the man who is shot has been virtually asking for it since the beginning of the yarn."[6] Similarly, *The Washington Daily News* also referred to this death; cheekily, they wrote "no one is any the worse for wear excepting Mr. Monroe Owsley, the blackmailing editor of a tabloid scandal sheet, who is used to abuse."[7] In fact, no reviewers had any sympathy for Tod being killed off in the movie. *Picture Play Magazine* even light-heartedly refers to Owsley as "the columnist who is conveniently bumped off."[8]

Tod's fate starts to be spelled out for him when he attempts to blackmail a crooked guy, Stoney Stone, and his affair with a married woman. Stoney threatens to kill him. Later in the movie, when Gerry and Buster are enjoying an engagement party, the men play a "murder" game. Jokes are pointed toward Tod. During the game, Buster's father reveals that Tod has threatened to expose Gerry's past in his gossip magazine.

When Tod shows up dead, the suspicion falls on Buster. He's cleared when it turns out that Stoney is the real murderer, leaving Gerry and Buster to enjoy their happily ever after.

Sally Eilers, Owsley, and Ginger Rogers in Hat Check Girl. *©20th Century Fox (courtesy Everett Collection)*

Hat Check Girl received fairly decent reviews, but it wasn't considered to be anything exceptional. Rian James, the author who wrote the original novel of the same name, expressed dissatisfaction with the film adaptation, noting that after the first third, it barely resembles the story he had written. Interestingly, the novel version of Owsley's character was much different. Instead of a villain, "our Tod Reese was a swell, big-hearted newspaper leg-man."[9]

Hat Check Girl was nearly lost forever (perhaps to James's great pleasure). For decades, it went unseen by the masses. In 2013, the Museum of Modern Art's Department of Film collaborated with Twentieth Century Fox to restore and preserve a rare print of the movie.[10] The picture was given a screening at Turner Classic Movies' Classic Film Festival in 2014. Since then, it has only had selected screenings and no mass release in a modern format for fans to easily watch. Maybe that will change one day.

THE MARCH OF YOUTH. Vibrantly it goes across the screens of the world, parading the spirit by which that world shall ever be remade. Here are four jaunty fellows on the Fox lot, linked in a vigorous goose-step across the grounds. From West to East: Phillips Holmes, Monroe Owsley, Ben Lyon and James Dunn.

Publicity piece in the October 8, 1932 issue of Motion Picture Herald.
(courtesy Media History Digital Library)

During Owsley's work on *Hat Check Girl,* he enjoyed a visit from his brother and sister-in-law who had traveled from El

Paso to see him. Photographs of Owsley with Anita Page at a movie premiere appeared in multiple newspapers. After *Hat Check Girl*'s release, the gossips focused on Owsley and Veree Teasdale. Owsley's interest in cars and car races garnered some attention too.

Most notably, he was cast in another film from Fox.

Call Her Savage released in late November. It was Clara Bow's big comeback after a public and humiliating legal battle with her secretary that culminated in a stay at a sanitarium. It would also be her second-to-last film before she retired from the movies permanently.

The movie is based on Tiffany Thayer's novel of the same name. As one might infer from the title alone, the premise of both the book and the film is racist toward Native Americans. An opening action sequence portrays Native Americans as vicious and bloodthirsty. The attack on the white travelers is considered punishment by God for leader Silas (Fred Kohler)'s adultery.

Years later, Silas's daughter (Estelle Taylor's Ruth Springer) falls for a Native American named Ronasa, played by Weldon Heyburn. After it's suggested that they'll make love, a stone engraving flashes on the screen.

"For I….am a jealous God, and visit the sins of the fathers upon the children unto the third and fourth generation…."

The third generation is Nasa "Dynamite" Springer, played by Bow. She's wild, temperamental, and prone to physical violence. Her friend, Moonglow (Gilbert Roland), is half-Native, half-white, and all too generous and understanding toward Nasa, even when she hits him. Nasa's father (Willard Robertston) sends her away to Chicago to reform her. She graduates from her boarding school after two years, and she's set to make her debut in society by throwing a party.

Meanwhile, Owsley makes his first appearance as Larry Crosby, a rich pleasure-seeker. He abuses and breaks up with his girlfriend, Sunny De Lane (Thelma Todd), accusing her of cheating on him. "I'm afraid you don't deserve me, darling," he says to Sunny.

While leaving Sunny for Nasa, Sunny retorts that he'll come back to her and infers that he's also a chronic cheater. This is confirmed while Larry dances with Nasa. "I doubt there's any sin on the calendar I haven't been guilty of," he quips to the smitten woman.

Clara Bow and Owsley exchanging flirts on the dance floor in Call Her Savage. *©20th Century Fox (courtesy Everett Collection)*

They marry the next day, which causes Nasa's father to disown her. Larry later admits to marrying Nasa only to get even with Sunny for "double-crossing" him. Nasa goes on a gambling and spending spree with Larry's money as revenge, surrounding herself with luxury goods and men.

After a while, Larry's lawyer arrives at Nasa's home, claiming her husband is dying. She agrees to see him. The doctor warns his medical staff not to leave Larry and Nasa unattended. Once she's alone with Larry, he tries to rape her. She successfully fights him off and knocks him unconscious.

Bow turning her head from the vile creature her husband has turned into in Call Her Savage. *(courtesy Media History Digital Library)*

After the assault, the doctor informs her under very vague terms that Larry's mind has been affected by syphilis. Nasa worries, but not for herself or him. Instead, she's concerned for her unborn baby. The baby winds up being born two months premature, but the infant's in good health.

Though Larry and his money is now out of Nasa's life forever, her troubles worsen. When the baby gets sick, Nasa turns to sex work to buy medicine, but the baby passes away in a fire while she's gone. In a moment of tragic irony, Nasa receives a visit from Moonglow, who informs her that her grandfather (the sinful man who started it all) has passed and left her an enormous fortune.

Nasa later meets a millionaire's son, Jay Randall, played by Anthony Jowitt. He conceals his background and acts as her hired male escort. After Jay's identity is revealed, the pair wish to marry, but everything is ruined at a dinner party that has Larry and Sunny in attendance. All Nasa can do afterward is drink and think of the men who have traumatized her.

When Nasa gets word that her mother is dying, she rushes back home to Texas. There, it is revealed that Nasa is the secret daughter of Ronasa. This revelation allows her to finally understand who she is and possibly embrace Moonglow as her true love.

Call Her Savage received decent reviews from critics. Nearly all of the praise went to Bow, understandably, since it was her vehicle. Bow gives one of her most dynamic performances as Nasa, showcasing a wide range of intense emotions. Though the picture leaves much to be desired in terms of what the audience is supposed to take away from the story, there's never a dull moment in the film.

Owsley also delivers one of his best performances as a villain. He channels a previously unseen darkness into Larry during the assault. Much of the class Owsley usually exudes disappears as he transforms into a monster. The script and direction pushed the actor to show all the ugly sides an abusive husband can have.

An unexpected progressive moment in the movie involves one of Nasa and Jay's dates. They go to a type of gay bar in Greenwich Village, a pansy bar. This is one of the earliest portrayals of queer people in American cinema. The effeminate male performers dress as maids while they sing and dance to entertain the guests. Two women are shown during the whimsical song, and one is more masculine-coded and sitting quite close to her partner. A fight erupts in the bar, but it's not due to anyone's sexuality.

It would have been impossible to make a movie like *Call Her Savage* two years later, when the Motion Picture Production Code (also known as the Hays Code) censorship became strictly enforced. Nasa has several revealing outfits, the pansy bar is blatantly queer, and everything about Larry is a "don't" in the Code.

Newspapers and fan magazines alike were agog about the fight between Nasa and Sunny in the picture. Rumors claimed that Todd had decided the fight would be her only chance to steal a scene from Bow. "According to the script, Monroe Owsley was supposed to separate them. But Monroe was paralyzed by the intensity of the storm, weaving before and around him."[11]

When watching the actual scene in question, Owsley immediately tries to restrain Bow. The fight also doesn't match up with the claims that Todd kicked Bow in the stomach so hard that the latter "slumped to the ground." If such an explosive scuffle did occur, it's not the one that made it to the screen.

Another interesting piece of behind-the-scenes gossip reached *Motion Picture* magazine. "After one long and ardent kiss from Monroe Owsley, they tell Clara remarked, 'That was wonderful!' Responded Mr. Owsley courteously, 'Thank you. I enjoyed it myself.'"[12]

During December and January, Owsley shot two films with Warner Bros. that released in the spring of 1933. While filming, Louella Parsons reported in her column that "Monroe told me he had been on the wagon for a year and that he is getting pretty fed up on always breaking the Volstead act but he shouldn't care as long as he is such a success."[13]

The first of the simultaneously produced movies was a comedy-drama with Kay Francis and George Brent as the leads. *The Keyhole* follows Francis's Anne Brooks, a former dancer who is now a married woman with two husbands. One husband, Schuyler Brooks (Henry Kolker), is suspicious of his wife's fidgety ways. She's acting suspicious, however, because she's being blackmailed by her first husband.

As suspected, Owsley played the blackmailing husband, ex-dancer Maurice Le Brun. He even bore a mustache that seems more hideous than the one in *Indiscreet*. That mustache plus excessive amount of eye makeup and overly greased back hair instantly signals to the audience he's the bad guy, in case they weren't familiar with Owsley's face. To top it off, the movie opens with Maurice threatening to kill himself if Anne doesn't see him.

"You don't answer telephone calls, only suicide notes," Maurice wryly tells Anne after agreeing to finally divorce her for fifty thousand dollars, a sum she can't possibly gather without Schuyler knowing. Then Maurice has the nerve to proposition her. It merits him a well-deserved slap that rings with a clear smack. "The next time you try to kill yourself, let me know," Anne cooly remarks. "I'd love to help you."

Owsley, his fake mustache, and Kay Francis in Twin Husbands. *(courtesy Everett Collection)*

Anne seeks help from her second husband's sister (Helen Ware). Portia plots to have Anne lure Maurice to Havana.

Confidently, Portia claims she can get Maurice's visa cancelled, thus preventing him from returning to America.

Meanwhile, Schuyler has decided to hire a private detective to follow his wife while she goes to Cuba, despite claiming he trusts Anne. Neil Davis (Brent) is a jaded man who makes his living exposing two-timing women. As part of the investigation, Neil attempts to start a romance with Anne on the cruise ship to Havana.

Maurice follows Anne to Cuba, as expected. Not so expected (except to the audience) is the fact that Neil finds himself genuinely falling for Anne during his sleuthing.

The climax of the picture begins with Neil confessing to Anne about his profession and his feelings. While he leaves to deal with Schuyler, a heated (and possibly drunk) Maurice enters Anne's room and attacks her. Maurice ends up falling to his death, and Anne ends her relationship with Schuyler. All obstacles toward Neil and Anne's relationship are neatly cleared with the film's last few minutes.

The Keyhole generated fairly positive reviews. Despite a low budget, *The Keyhole* does its best to look glamorous. Francis and Brent both bring pure class to their roles. The film uses large, expensive-looking sets, and Francis went through an astonishing twenty-three costume changes with gowns provided by Orry-Kelly. Professional gold digger, Glenda Farrell's Dot, also looks magnificent as she fleeces Neil's naïve partner (Allen Jenkins) for every cent he has in an amusing side plot.

Antonio Moreno had initially been cast as Maurice, but Owsley replaced him when the studio decided to switch up roles, including swapping William Powell for Brent. Owsley's scenes are few, but his presence is strong enough to leave an impression. He might not have had much acting to do, but his caddish mustache is unforgettable.

Owsley is fortunately clean faced for his role in *Ex-Lady*, starring Bette Davis and Gene Raymond. Davis played Helen

Bauer, a commercial illustrator who believes marriage ruins love. Raymond played her lover who runs an advertising agency, Don Peterson.

The movie opens with Helen breaking up a party at her house. Owsley's Nick Malvyn is clearly enamored with Helen and tries his hardest stay overnight. Once she gets him and the other guests out, Don sneaks back in using the key to Helen's apartment that he has. The pair have been lovers for a while—Don wants to marry her, but Helen opposes it, liking their current arrangement.

Helen finally agrees to marriage after Don persists in his proposal. She also joins Don's advertising agency as their illustrator, even though Nick had a more lucrative job offer for her. After a blissful honeymoon, the married couple return to work where the agency is doing poorly.

At a party, Helen and Don's relationship starts to fracture. Married woman Peggy Smith (Kay Strozzi) has eyes on Don, and Helen notices how cozy they're getting. Then, Helen confesses to Don that she's working on drawings for the lucrative agency during her off-hours. Hurt, Don takes up Peggy's offer for a date, which Helen discovers.

Helen's fears of marriage ruining the relationship seems to have come true, so she proposes they live as "lovers" again, implying they could see other people. The arrangement seems to be working until Helen and Don attempt dating other people. They reunite in the end, content to be a married couple.

The pre-release publicity boasted that *Ex-Lady* was to make Davis into a star, but it failed short of its goal. Many critics panned *Ex-Lady*, and Davis herself considered it one of her worst films. "It is a part of my career that my conscious tastefully avoids," she wrote in *The Lonely Life*. [14]"I only recall that from the daily shooting to the billboards, falsely picturing me half-naked, my shame was only exceeded by my fury."

Bette Davis reluctantly kissing Owsley in Ex-Lady. *She hated this film. (courtesy Everett Collection)*

Though some reviews sympathized with Davis for the concept she had been given, there were few praises for her acting. Her numerous scenes in bed or kissing someone were painted in a negative light. Raymond received the most positive attention from the film. "It is Gene Raymond's everlasting credit that he alone survived the preview without bringing forth a snicker upon himself," wrote *The Hollywood Reporter* in their review.[15]

It's a shame most audiences at the time saw the film's provocativeness as something cheap and crude. The movie suffers from too many empty scenes where little is happening, but the overall story is still quite modern and asks the audience to challenge their conceptions of love and marriage. Raymond himself seemed to enjoy the movie. "I felt the film was ahead of its time and that Bette looked just wonderful in it," he told Lawrence J. Quirk.[16]

Little was written in reviews about Owsley, whom Bette Davis described as "marvelously corrupt" in her autobiography. His role wasn't inherently different from the caddish heavies he had been playing, but *Ex-Lady* gave Owsley many chances to demonstrate a lustful side without a glass of alcohol in his hand. His character's eyes are only ever on Helen, and his intentions are clear with every line out of his mouth. *Ex-Lady*'s most interesting shot is toward the end when Nick pulls Helen to the floor and embraces her in a passionate kiss, surrounded by furs and luxurious pillows. Nick's face when Helen ditches him before they can go any further is comical but not over the top.

Quirk wrote in *Fasten Your Seatbelts* that Davis acknowledged Owsley's abilities as an actor. "Davis, while she admitted that 'this rat-faced rodent gives me the shivers,' was the first to concede that whatever [Owsley] projected, it was consummately effective on camera."[17]

Owsley also had praises for Davis, as the *New York Sun* reported. "She's grand to work with, gets right into the part, makes you do it. She's got something, that girl."[18]

In that same article, when it came to his character's strong seduction methods, Owsley doubted his character would have actually coerced Davis's character into sex.

"In that scene where he tells her he's locked the door and thrown the key in the well, I think he's only kidding. I think he's the kind of fellow who might kid right up to the last minute but who really wasn't a bad sort at all. Or do you think he meant it?"

That is up to the audience's interpretation.

After Owsley finished shooting *The Keyhole* and *Ex-Lady*, he departed for a long visit home. He had grown tired of Hollywood again—and he had gotten into a scandal.

CHAPTER SIX

January of 1933 brought news that Monroe Owsley was buying orchids for Jean Harlow and escorting her to night clubs—and that he was being sued by a twenty-one-year-old studio employee and pianist named Catherine Allen.[1]

The charge was a breach of promise in marriage. Allen claimed that Owsley had proposed marriage in October, which she had accepted, but he later refused to marry her, prompting her to sue him for trifling with her affections. Some reports claimed Allen sued him for $50,000 dollars, while others brought up $75,000 dollars. Many papers were quick to compare the lawsuit with Owsley's on screen roles.

It was at the same time that Owsley hopped in his "special built Cord, a wicked looking monster with blue leather upholstering and nickel gadgets"[2] with Julian Fowlkes. Fowlkes was a film director who had just finished some work on a few of Shirley Temple's earliest shorts.

On their way back to the East Coast, Owsley and Fowlkes attended a bull fight in Mexico. The *Richmond Times-Dispatch* reported that Owsley, "who always takes the heavy view of things,"[3] rooted for the bull and even offered to buy it. The bull noticeably didn't join the two for the rest of their journey.

The pair also stopped in Texas to visit Owsley's brother and sister-in-law. While they were in El Paso, journalist Betty Luther interviewed Owsley, who didn't hesitate to express his frustrations with Hollywood.

"As usual, I didn't get the girl," he said about his roles in *The Keyhole* and *Ex-Lady*. "That's the trouble with the movies—they cast you as a type. You can never get away from it. You stay in a rut. I'm tired of it."

After proclaiming himself as a rather decent sort, he made a somber observation about his career. "You can't get a following playing the cad."[4]

On February 6, Owsley and Fowlkes stopped in Knoxville, Tennessee since their car was "out of whack."[5] The pair enjoyed a chat with staff from the newspaper, who met the Hollywood travelers while Owsley was shaving and running water for a bath. Owsley and Fowlkes commented that they loved the beauty of Knoxville, and both men expressed an interest to eventually retire in the city surrounded by the Great Smoky Mountains. The article writer, Herbert Barrier, Jr., commented that he had never seen an actor like Owsley who was so interested in the local scene, including the football team.

When the conversation turned to the movies, Owsley found his frustrations being echoed by Barrier. Owsley's resentment toward his roles had led him to visit his parents, and he claimed to be considering a play in New York or London.

The article was more amusing than anything, though, and it offered a rare insight on Owsley's friendships. A humorous autographed picture of Frederic March, whom Owsley said was one of his best friends, was found while the staff looked for a photograph to use in the newspaper. "'March at Work,' the writing on the picture said. March was lying flatly and supinely at ease, eyes closed."

A few days later, Owsley and Fowlkes encountered an embarrassing situation in Roanoke, Virginia. The pair had dallied too long during their trip and used up all their travelers checks, leaving them unable to buy gasoline when the tank ran low.

Between the two of them, they had $17,500 in cashier's checks. Owsley tried to get a hundred dollars in cash with a new cashier's check for the remainder, but the bankers declined this option. The actor couldn't write a personal check, either, since he had transferred all of his remaining cash to a savings account in Greenwich Village.

Owsley ended up having to wire his parents in New York for money. A return wire came later that night, followed by a call from his father.

The car experienced more troubles the next day, breaking down near Buchanan, and the pair had to stay in Roanoke for an additional day.

The article didn't end without a little bit of speculation on Owsley's love life. When asked about a photograph of himself with Anita Page, the actor responded, "Oh, they snap all sorts of pictures in Hollywood!"[6]

Owsley stayed out East until mid-April, looking over a number of plays for the stage and playing around with some reporters at the *New York Times*. Then he decided to head back to California for a possible film deal (and maybe court). On his way, he drove to Richmond, Virginia to visit Fowlkes. Fowlkes was now directing the pageant for the city's Beaux Arts Ball.

Though Owsley claimed to be tired and didn't want to talk about anything, he "naturally gravitated" to a newspaper shop in Richmond. His interest in his old newspaper days hadn't faded.

"I haven't forgotten that I once did some writing, and like everyone who has done any at all, I think that some day I'll write more," he said.[7]

He later stopped in El Paso to visit his brother and sister-in-law. By this time, he had race car driver Jimmy Trippe as a traveling companion. While in El Paso, Owsley spoke with a reporter and apparently had love on his mind. He admitted to having "a girl on the [California] coast" he couldn't forget.

"I didn't fall in love while I was in the east. I suppose I'm doomed to be the third person in a love affair."[8]

In May, *New Movie* reported Owsley was back in town, driving "a cream-colored roadster with red leather upholstery."[9]

That same month, he signed with Columbia Pictures for *Brief Moment*. As shooting started, Catherine Allen dropped her lawsuit with Owsley. If there was an out-of-court settlement, the amount was never publicly revealed.[10]

Anita Page, aviator Art Goebel, and Owsley at the Los Angeles Air Races. From Modern Screen, *October 1933. (courtesy Media History Digital Library)*

Owsley had quite a few mentions in the press that summer regarding his personal activities. He was often seen with Anita Page, as her father seemed to trust him with her. She attended the Los Angeles Air Races with him in addition to being his date to the theater or his dancing partner. Owsley also attended auto races with Lew Ayres and Ginger Rogers. An El Paso woman named Frances Miller passed a screen test in California, and Owsley had been instrumental in getting her before the cameras.

His reputation for drinking on-screen, and likely off-screen, grew to the point that columnists made quips about Owsley's drinking. A couple of writers joked that Owsley was thankful he didn't have a hangover on June 21 since it was the longest day of the year. Harrison Carroll later wrote that the joke had prompted a few people to wire Owsley with concern.

His association with alcohol wasn't helped by *Brief Moment*'s release in September. In the movie, he plays Harold "Sig" Sigrift, a jobless pleasure seeker who is more than happy to drink and sponge money off his best friend.

The movie reunited Owsley with Gene Raymond, who plays rich playboy Rodney Deane. This time, Owsley and Raymond's characters are best friends instead of romantic rivals. Though Sig alludes to trying to win Rod's fiancée (Carole Lombard's Abby Fane) in the past, Owsley's character has no sexual interest in the leading woman. Sig's partying ways, however, cause friction between Rod and Abby.

Brief Moment opens with Rod introducing Abby to his wealthy family who are concerned about their position in society. Rod's parents and brother (Donald Cook) disapprove of Rod marrying a woman they consider out of their class, but the marriage happens anyway.

The pair enjoy a honeymoon in Europe and come home to an apartment furnished by Sig, dashing Abby's hope to create their own home. The Deanes have also given Rodney some of their household staff and provide him with a generous allowance of four thousand dollars a month. With little in his affluent life changing except for a wife, Rod continues partying and gambling with Abby, Sig, and his other friends every night.

The only person concerned with their lifestyle is Abby. Sig is still happy to use Rod's money, and he even boasts about his easy life. While drinking and waiting for Rod to get more money from his father, Sig says, "You know, it positively gets on my nerves to see people working. I'll be on edge for days."

Irene Ware, Owsley, Carole Lombard, Arthur Hohl, and Gene Raymond in Brief Moment. *Note the way Owsley and Lombard are looking at each other. (courtesy Everett Collection)*

After six months, Abby grows tired of the constant playing. She's ashamed of Rod's alcohol consumption and his refusal to make a dollar for himself. Her relationship with Sig also grows antagonistic. Jealousy and heartbreak brews inside her when Sig whisks Rod away during one of the married couple's rare nights at home alone, causing Abby and Rod to fight.

Abby then asks Rod's father (Reginald Mason) to cut him off and make him less spoiled. "So far, my marriage has been one long drunk," she explains, but her concerns are ignored.

To pacify Abby, Rod goes to his father and asks for a job at their family business. Rod agrees to start from the bottom, but he quickly finds the life of a paper pusher isn't for him. A few weeks later, he discovers his brother Frank doesn't do anything but play as a vice-president of the company. Rod quits working and starts spending his days with Sig at the race tracks, but he doesn't tell his wife.

For a month, Rod misleads Abby about what he's really doing during the day. When Abby discovers the truth, she leaves Rod and goes back to her job at the night club. Time goes by, Rod realizes that Sig is no friend of his, and he hits the streets to look for a real job.

When Rod earns his first salary, he goes to Abby, who takes him back. "I suppose you'll nag me until I get a raise," Rod comments. "Why not?" Abby tearfully asks. "You're worth more." The movie ends with them kissing each other.

Brief Moment had been a success on Broadway during the 1931-1932 season. Its translation to the screen with lots of beautiful, soft lighting and dozens of gorgeous outfits for Lombard generated many positive reviews. The actors themselves bring their characters to life with a great deal of panache and dramatically appropriate flaws.

Lombard is certainly the heart of the film, and it's hard not to wonder if her own cratered marriage to William Powell reflected in her acting. After filming *Brief Moment,* Lombard went to Reno and obtained a divorce from Powell.

Owsley's role as the toxic best friend is interesting and differs from his other drunken cad roles. The tension between Abby and Sig has the same story beats as a romantic rivalry for Rod's affections, and Sig ultimately "loses" the guy when Rod chooses Abby and hard work over Sig and extravagant pleasure.

Most of the film's humor rests on Owlsey's shoulders, which he delivered with the type of classy shamelessness that he had mastered over the years. At the beginning of the movie, Sig is obviously more interested in the possible drama that would happen from Rod marrying Abby than anything else. Later, when greeting the married couple back from their honeymoon, he effortlessly bluffs his way through security. "Would you let me through? I'm meeting the Spanish ambassador." Sig's drunken scenes are also played in the familiar comedic Owsley style.

Owsley received a lot of attention that fall in Hollywood gossip columns. He was linked to Barbara Pepper, Bobbe Arnst, Claire Windsor, Muriel Evans, and Vivian Tobin. Frequently, he could be spotted at popular high society spots such as the Cocoanut Grove and Beverly Wilshire Hotel's Gold Room. He even refereed a few boxing/wrestling bouts during a great stadium show put on by Safeway Stores, Inc.[11]

Sometime during the same period, Owsley filmed a picture with an independent production company, William Berke. This time, he would be the leading man and "get the girl."

In *The Woman Who Dared,* Owsley played a newspaper reporter named Jack Goodwin opposite Claudia Dell's Mickey Martin, a textile plant owner that produces corsets and similar garments.

Mickey takes over the factory after her father dies, and she refuses to pay off racketeers for "protection." After repeated bomb threats at her factory, she partners up with Jack, who quits his job to help her. A romance develops between them while they round up evidence to put the gang away forever.

Early previews of *The Woman Who Dared* were screened in late November and received positive attention.[12] It later hit general theaters in 1934, although not many due to it being an indie film. The enforcement of the Hays Code probably didn't help its chances at getting shown in more theaters. A film still of *The Woman Who Dared* shows Lola Lane and a few other women modeling underwear in front of a crowd. It's safe to assume there are more moments of various states of undress.

Only known film still from The Woman Who Dared. *Lola Lane models in the center. Owsley and Claudia Dell are watching from the left. (courtesy Library of Congress)*

Frustratingly, little is known about the movie today. As an indie production, it didn't receive the same press coverage that the major studios had. Once it left theaters, it wasn't ever publicly seen again.

The Woman Who Dared was thought to be a lost film until 2005. *The Daily Telegraph* reported that a nitrate print of the movie had been discovered in an aircraft hanger in England along with hundreds of other lost or unseen films.[13] No further news has been announced about *The Woman Who Dared,* so the current status of the nitrate print is unknown. It's possible it might be too damaged to preserve any content, given the delicate and flammable nature of nitrate.

With little coverage for *The Woman Who Dared,* Owsley was unable to change his image as a cad or ne'er-do-well. It almost seems cruel that modern audiences today are deprived of the chance to see him as a romantic lead and give us the chance to determine if he had the ability to play the hero he wanted to be.

It was back to the caddish roles for the frustrated actor.

CHAPTER SEVEN

1934 was a busy year in the movies for Monroe Owsley. Between playing tennis—where an observing writer cracked, "That guy hits every ball as though it were a second-act curtain!" [1]—and frequenting Al Levy's Tavern for tailored meals, Owsley worked on seven films that year.

Prohibition had been repealed officially in the United States on December 5, 1933, which meant that Owsley's theory of playing less drunks in films would be tested.

Invincible Pictures's *Twin Husbands* released in late February as a vehicle for the charismatic John Miljan. Miljan, like Owsley, had been typecast as villains through his screen career, although his heavies were more suave and imposing. For *Twin Husbands,* Miljan had wanted the chance to prove he could do comedy and play a romantic character, so he offered to act without remuneration.[2]

He did so well, though, that producer Maury Cohen didn't hold Miljan to his original offer and made sure he was paid for his work. Cohen was a producer notable for pushing the allowance of double features in theatres. Seeing two movies for the price of one scored a huge hit in the Great Depression era of America. Though it immediately benefited independent studios like Invincible Pictures, major studios also began producing more B movies for double features.

Miljan played Jerry Van Trevor, the victim to a kidnapping. When Jerry awakens at the start of the film, he has no idea whose fancy house he's in, but he keeps calm and investigates. A man proclaiming to be his butler Greyson (Wilson Benge) enters the room and addresses him as Jerry Werrenden, the owner of the estate. He references a wife, Chloe (Shirley Grey), whose existence surprises Jerry.

Jerry attacks Greyson and gets him to reveal what's really going on, since Jerry knows he's not an amnesiac. Greyson confesses to being a character actor, and Jerry recruits him to his side. Jerry's "wife" enters the room next. Chloe pulls a gun on him when he tries to play husband to her. At this point, Jerry grabs the gun, and the movie's main antagonist enters the room.

Owsley played Colton Drain, the secretary to the real Jerry Werrenden. Colton admits to abducting Jerry since he looks identical to Chloe's missing husband. The pair wish to use Jerry to obtain $200,000 in bonds during a meeting with a man known as Colonel Gordon Lewis (Hale Hamilton). Jerry acquiesces, presumably because he has no other choice. But when the Colonel shows up, Jerry baffles Colton and Chloe by inviting him to stay for the night.

A series of nonstop twists and turns begin at this point. Two thieves break into the house, but they find Colton already trying to open the safe. Jerry enters, and one of the thieves recognizes him as a notorious, but honorable safecracker called "The Sparrow." When the police show up, Colton has Jerry arrested for stealing the bonds. They take both Jerry and Chloe away for further questioning. Then, the *real* police show up.

Owsley, Shirley Grey, and John Miljan trying to figure each other out in Twin Husbands. *(courtesy Everett Collection)*

Jerry had planned everything up to this point, and he uses his time alone with Chloe to both flirt with her and find out why she agreed to Colton's plot. She reveals her husband had treated her like a dog, and she wanted the money to start over. Determined to get to the bottom of the case, Jerry investigates Colton's office, where he discovers a telegram that reveals the real Jerry Werrenden had passed away in an accident—a fact that Colton had conveniently hid.

When Colton and the real police find Jerry and Chloe again, Colton's schemes blow up in his face. Chloe asserts that Jerry is her real husband, and Jerry secretly shows his evidence of Colton's wrongdoing. He advises Colton take a one way trip to South America, which Colton agrees to do, knowing facing the law is his only other outcome.

Jerry and Chloe, who are quite into each other now, are left alone. In the end, Jerry decides to trade in his shady past for a more honest future with his new love.

Twin Husbands earned positive reviews from critics, but the film ultimately failed to transform Miljan into any kind of comedic hero. He would continue to play heavies and people of significant authority for most of his long career.

Owsley and Miljan had good chemistry as two crooks trying to outwit each other. Owsley's signature sneer filled the screen multiple times, and he conveys masterful shamelessness when Colton realizes he's lost the battle. "I always did want to see South America."

The next picture Owsley worked on brought him back to Fox's studio. *Wild Gold* starred John Boles as Steve Miller, a smitten construction engineer, and Claire Trevor as Jerry Jordan, a singer in a Reno nightclub with a horrible husband. As expected, that husband was played by one Monroe Owsley.

Walter Jordan's seedy ways are revealed almost instantly in the film. Two detectives show up after Jerry's number in the club; Walter is in trouble for conning five thousand dollars from a woman. The detectives order the married couple to leave. Jerry, who's had enough of her husband's schemes and lies, leaves Walter and heads to San Francisco.

On her way, she meets a club guest who had been annoyingly pursuing her—Steve Miller. Some shenanigans ensue with Steve deservedly sinking his car in a river after pestering Jerry. Steve hitches a ride from J. "Jake" Lorillard Pushkin (Harry Green) and his Golden Girls, a troupe of dancers seeking fame. Dixie Belle (Ruth Gillette) drives them to Red Rock, a town that's filled with gold prospectors thanks to the rising price of gold.

Jerry's car breaks down near a gold prospector known as Pop Benson (Roger Imhof). He offers to have her stay with him until her car's fixed. Unfortunately, Steve is also a friend of Pop's, and he's *also* staying with Pop. When Steve tries to make a move on Jerry, she knocks him unconscious.

She nurses him back to health, and Steve's feelings for Jerry are inexplicably reciprocated. When Steve gets a job working for the bridge being built in San Francisco (the future Golden Gate Bridge), Jerry decides to get a divorce from her no-good husband so she can be with Steve.

As if to speak of the devil, Walter shows up in Red Rock, looking for Jerry. He loots a bag of gold from Pop in the process, and Pop catches him. Their confrontation leads to Pop's death. Walter disappears from the scene.

After finding Pop's body, everyone also immediately becomes aware that Pop's gold has been stolen. Law enforcement starts searching everyone. Jerry, Steve, and Jake want to send Pop's body to Connecticut, where he has family. Jake suggests they put on a show to raise the funds necessary for it.

Dixie, meanwhile, meets Walter. They had apparently been involved with each other some time ago and make plans to leave town together.

While the show is on, Jerry realizes Walter is in town. She begs Walter to leave, but he extorts her for money. Jake, meanwhile, decides to gamble to raise the rest of the money needed for Pop's funeral in Connecticut. He loses it all.

Jerry later tells Steve about Walter while in Pop's cabin. Dixie then rushes into the cabin with the stolen bag of gold. Walter had planted it among her belongings and had planned to frame her for the theft.

It becomes clear that Walter is responsible for Pop's death. Jerry rushes to Walter's side and begs him to leave, but not for his sake—she wants to prevent Steve from becoming a murderer. Steve quickly shows up, looking for a fight.

Conveniently, a storm destroys the town's dam, and a flood wipes out Red Rock. Walter is among the number of people who die during the catastrophe. This leaves Jerry and Steve free to head for their life together in San Francisco.

Wild Gold received mixed reviews. The film's flood scene

detracted from the story for many people. An act of nature didn't provide a satisfying conclusion to the characters' various dilemmas. It does, indeed, seem like an odd way to get rid of Owsley's character. In the movie, Jerry says a divorce would take six weeks, which isn't a lengthy amount of time to wait.

Furthermore, was Pop's body ever sent to his family? The movie doesn't say.

There are good moments to *Wild Gold,* though, and it's a decent watch. The most interesting part of the movie is Red Rock itself. Much of the filming took place in Kernville, California. Actual amateur gold prospectors were offered the chance to work in *Wild Gold.* The gold rushers were paid a tiny sum to film various scenes, giving Red Rock a feeling of an authentic rustic town.

Despite the fairly weak script, the film's cast performed adequately. Green and Gillette carried the bulk of the comedy, leaving Owsley to focus on being the film's villain. There's nothing particularly special about his acting in this role, though. It almost feels like the director hadn't given him much direction for his scenes. Still, Owsley effectively portrays the role given to him with his face alone.

Though he could have used more scenes in *Wild Gold,* Owsley is blatantly underutilized in his role for Universal's *Little Man, What Now?*

Based on the German novel by Hans Fallada, the story revolves around a couple suffering to get by in their harsh life. Early 1930s Germany was in a fragile political situation. When Adolf Hitler took over in 1933, the novel had to undergo revisions to remove negative portrayals of the Nazis. The American version of *Little Man, What Now?* was able to adapt the story a little more faithfully than the heavily censored German film from 1933. But due to the Motion Picture Production Code's own reluctance to paint the Nazis in a bad light, the script still misses much of the original novel's themes.

Little Man, What Now? starred Margaret Sullavan and Douglass Montgomery. Montgomery's Johannes "Hans" Pinneberg marries Sullivan's Emma "Lämmchen" Morschel after they discover she's pregnant. From there, the couple have to embark on various ups and downs as they aim to build a life together for their child, scrambling for every mark possible in a poor economy.

Owsley played a very minor role in the film, but his character manages to be annoying throughout his limited screen time. Kessler is one of the salesmen working with Hans, and he instigates a fight when he reveals that Hans's stepmother has been running a brothel in her house. Kessler is quick to recover from Hans attacking him, calmly adjusting his tie as though he were used to causing such trouble.

Douglass Montgomery, Alan Mowbray, and Owsley in Little Man, What Now? *(courtesy Everett Collection)*

Though *Little Man, What Now?* received much praise from critics, it proved to be a box office disappointment. The film's heavy story might have been unappealing to Great Depression-era audiences seeking escapism. Most of the box office successes in 1934 involved wealthy characters in romantic affairs, like *It Happened One Night,* or were spectacular epics, such as *Cleopatra.*

It still holds up as a fascinating film. Maybe not a great Owsley film, but it makes for a poignant watch.

While working on *Wild Gold* and *Little Man, What Now?,* news of Owsley's engagement to the daughter of a prominent Los Angeles realty dealer, Katherine Toberman, filled multiple papers across the country. Articles speculated a summer wedding, and Louella Parsons gushed that Owsley was so happy over his approaching marriage to Toberman.[3]

However, the person most surprised by the announcement appeared to have been Toberman herself.[4] She immediately denied the engagement altogether and claimed that the romance between them had ended. Unlike the broken engagement with Yvonne Grey, Owsley made no public statements. He left the Tobermans to do the talking.

Hollywood magazine reported another court case for Owsley that spring.[5] A "fashionable tailoring firm" had summoned the actor to make him pay for an expensive overcoat. Owsley argued that since he already had five, he didn't need a sixth. The argument seemed to be enough for the judge who ruled in Owsley's favour.

Owsley began work in the spring and summer for more films. These movies would release after July 1, which was officially a new era in Hollywood—one of enforced censorship.

CHAPTER EIGHT

Back in 1915, the Supreme Court had ruled that films weren't entitled to legal protection for free speech, likening the film industry to other businesses. After numerous scandals in the early 1920s, including the much publicized trial of Roscoe Arbuckle, studio executives elected to start regulating the content in their films. This led to William H. Hays giving up his cabinet position in Warren G. Harding's presidency and taking the chairman position for Motion Picture Producers and Distributors of America. He oversaw the formation of the Motion Picture Production Code, which is also known as the Hays Code.

A list of "don'ts" and "be carefuls" were key points in the Code, but the Hays office didn't have the authority to actually censor any content yet. They instead had to appeal to studios to remove questionable content. This changed in 1934 with the establishment of the Production Code Administration.

All films released on or after July 1, 1934 had to get a seal of approval from the PCA. While some films were released by smaller studios without any kind of seal of approval, they had to contend with local laws about if their content was suitable for viewings in theaters. Those pictures often were limited in distribution. In addition to the tightened censorship of new films, several pre-Code movies were removed from theaters and not allowed to be shown again until they were edited or remade altogether to match the PCA's standards.

Monroe Owsley's first Hays code era movie was Monogram Pictures's *Shock,* a World War I film about a British military officer who develops amnesia after an attack by the Germans. Ralph Forbes played the amnesiac Derek Marbury/John Drake. Owsley had the role of Bob Hayworth, Derek's mustachioed captain who's also romantically interested in Derek's wife, Lucy (Gwenllian Gill).

The film opens with artillery fire and explosions—and a wedding. Derek and Lucy have just gotten married. Derek teases Lucy about his captain who had been courting her for months. They've gotten married without informing the captain, even though Bob's brother Gilroy (Douglas Walton) was the best man at the wedding.

Bob learns the news, and the captain makes his first entrance of the film overhearing his soldiers making fun of him for losing Lucy. When the jokes are over and Derek is back from his short honeymoon, Gilroy gets assigned to a dangerous mission. Terrified, Gilroy is unable to handle the assignment, and Bob berates him for being scared. "You're not going to pull our name in the mud. Why do you suppose I had you sent to me in the first place?"

Gilroy kills himself soon after, leaving Bob and Derek to deal with his body. Bob coldly only thinks of the scandal it will cause him. To help avoid the Hayworth name being disgraced, Derek takes the body with him to make Gilroy's death look like a casualty of war. In the process, Derek gets hurt by German soldiers, far away from anyone who knew him. His wife is quickly informed that Derek has gone missing.

When Derek wakes up in a London hospital, he has no memories of his identity and is in a state of shell shock, the term used before post-traumatic stress disorder was officially recognized. He's given the name John Drake by a hospital attendant who doesn't appear to believe in amnesia. His first assignment out of the hospital is patrolling the streets of London, far from the actual battle. Bob recognizes him, but Derek ignores him when Bob calls out his name.

Bob starts spreading news that Derek may be a deserter, hoping to sway Lucy's heart toward him. This plan fails, as she believes there must be another reason Bob saw Derek in a different uniform.

Derek transfers to the front lines again, distinguishes himself in battle, and unwittingly befriend's Lucy's brother, Alan (Alex Courtney). Alan shows Derek a picture of Lucy with her young son, who had been conceived during the Marburys' short honeymoon. Through all of this, Derek experiences episodes of confusion, his past still a blank.

When Alan becomes fatally injured, Derek agrees to see Lucy and help find her missing husband. This brings him to Lucy's house as she turns down Bob's continued advances.

Bob and Derek pass each other as Derek enters. Lucy recognizes him instantly, but she doesn't reveal his identity and plays along with his search for her husband. During this time, Derek falls in love with Lucy again, and their son comes to admire him too.

After the pair kiss, Lucy tries to tell Derek who he really is, but Derek thinks her husband is standing between them. It upsets him greatly, and he makes plans to leave for Canada. Bob decides to cause some trouble out of spite and reveals who he is to Derek—but he actually ends up helping Derek recover his memories. Derek soon awakens at home. He's happily reunited with Lucy, and a bruised officer friend (Reginald Sharland) tells him he's been punching Bob in the nose.

Ralph Forbes remembering his identity after Owsley accidentally helped him in Shock. *(courtesy Everett Collection)*

Shock received mixed reviews with its weak story being the main source of criticism, although *Motion Picture Herald* was accidentally funny in warning audiences about most of the cast having a King's English accent.[1] One review in *The Buffalo News* humorously noted that "Monroe Owsley, usually a most disagreeable chap, unintentionally does Ralph Forbes a good turn in 'Shock' and reunites a family. That is probably the most surprising thing about 'Shock.'"[2]

Owsley (and his mustache) gave a standard performance, although his sleazy character lacked some bite. In fact, much of the film's acting and potentially deep themes come off as superficial, either because of poor directing or tighter self-censorship. Sorrow is barely expressed, despite there being many reasons for characters to cry. Lucy is unnervingly composed when discussing her missing husband and deceased brother, and Alan is cheerful as he dies. It's frankly a relief when Derek breaks down in front of Lucy, confused about his identity.

It was a novel idea to have the movie's villain be the reason the hero gets his memories back, but it failed to have the dramatic tension it should have had. *Shock* had plenty of good ideas but poor execution.

The buzz for Owsley's next film, *She Was a Lady,* included press articles about Owsley embracing his villainous character roles. Supposedly, he didn't want fan mail because it would mean that audiences weren't hating him enough.[3] Had Owsley actually come to accept his typecasting, or was it publicity drummed up by Fox?

She Was a Lady gave Owsley (and his mustache) the chance to work with Helen Twelvetrees again, though he would not have her heart in this film. Her leading man would instead be Donald Woods playing the rich playboy, Tommy Traill.

The film follows Sheila Vane (Twelvetrees), the daughter of a disinherited English aristocrat (Ralph Morgan). Her father had been disowned by his parents for marrying a family maid, and the Vanes now live in Montana. However, Stanley has regrets of his past, and he wishes for his daughter to return to England and claim her title.

Sheila gets a job as a riding instructor at a ranch, where she meets Tommy Traill. He falls for her instantly, but she refuses to marry him until he can prove himself.

Meanwhile, Sheila's father passes away. Sheila ends up joining a circus as a trick rider, where she encounters the circus's shady publicist, Jerry Couzins (Monroe Owsley). After saving up enough money and briefly reuniting with Tommy, Sheila finally goes to England. Her planned attempt to join the aristocratic family fails, though, since her aunt and uncle don't wish for anyone to know Sheila is the maternal granddaughter of the Vanes' family butler.

She returns to America—and to Tommy. Tommy introduces

her to his father, but the elder Traill refuses to acknowledge Sheila as a potential daughter-in-law due to her low class. Tommy and Sheila break up, and Sheila soon meets Jerry again. She agrees to take a job at the nightclub he runs.

Months later, Tommy appears in the club, and he fights with Jerry after Sheila lies about being engaged to Jerry. Sheila brings Tommy home, and his father at lasts wishes for Sheila to marry him, stating that her background no longer matters. All ends well for the couple.

She Was a Lady fared poorly on the review front. *The Film Daily*[4] blamed both the movie's director and the script's source material, a serial novelization of the same name by Elizabeth Cobb that had been published in *McCall's* magazine. Other reviews, however, praised Cobb's story and criticized the film adaptation itself. *She Was a Lady* had been one of McCall's most popular stories. Editors reported receiving around three thousand letters commenting on the story. Cobb herself was said to have opened more than fifteen hundred letters addressed to her directly.[5]

E. de S. Melcher, drama critic for Washington, D.C.'s *Evening Star,* revealed a behind-the-scenes moment of Owsley's acting for *She Was A Lady.* When Woods has to punch Owsley, he doesn't actually hit him. It was up to Owsley to make the punch seem real. "Have you ever tried throwing yourself backward into a bunch of chairs for no reason?" asked Melcher. "We must admit that Owsley does it very well."[6]

The Boston Globe wrote "the best piece of acting in the picture is done by the villain of the piece, Monroe Owsley."[7] All of those staged fights had paid off for him, at least.

Paramount Pictures's *Behold My Wife!* came out in December that year. The film's concept of a rich white man marrying an Apache woman to seek revenge against his prejudiced family unfortunately uses racist tropes about indigenous peoples. Sylvia

Sidney starred as Tonita Storm Cloud with Gene Raymond playing her leading man, Michael Carter.

The film quickly introduces the audience to the main cast of characters in Michael's inner circle. His family is concerned about the woman he plans to marry, and his married sister (Juliette Compton's Diana Curson) is having an affair with playboy Bob Prentice (Monroe Owsley). The family plots to interfere with the marriage, which leads to the woman jumping to her death. Diana and Bob are quick to hide their presence at the suicide scene.

When Michael finds out what has happened, he leaves his family in a fury. After driving recklessly for a while, he stumbles into a saloon and bonds with an Apache man named Pete (Dean Jagger) over drinks. Pete's girlfriend Tonita shows up, furious to see her boyfriend is drinking. Pete accidentally shoots Michael in the shoulder, and Tonita nurses Michael back to health in order to keep Pete out of trouble.

This action leads to her tribe disowning her. Michael hatches a plan to marry Tonita to make his family mad, but he doesn't let her know of the real reason behind his proposal. The couple marry and return to the Carters, but Michael keeps his distance from Tonita.

To his delight, Tonita has a tantrum in front of the paparazzi that greets them, and the Carters are mortified by their new family member. Diana decides to take control of the social situation by throwing a party for the newlyweds. She even convinces Tonita to put aside the Apache garments for a gown that she chose.

Meanwhile, it turns out Bob has missed a date with Diana. She quickly finds out that he broke their date in order to see another woman and threatens to kill him. "I'll do anything I please. Is that clear?" he tells her.

Michael explodes when he sees Tonita is the belle of the party and everyone adores her. In his rage, he reveals the real reason he married her, breaking her heart. Tonita decides to leave the party with Bob.

While Bob makes his move on Tonita, Diana shows up at his place. Bob refuses to take Diana back, even though she claims to have left her husband. During their argument, Diana shoots Bob, killing him instantly.

Tonita, seeing no reason to live, decides to confess to the crime and turns herself in to the police. But Michael arrives at the station and claims that he did it, determined to protect Tonita. He confesses he loves her when they're alone, and they embrace. Tonita tells Michael that Diana is Bob's killer, and the film ends with a shot of the police listening in to their conversation.

Though the film's treatment toward Apache people is regrettable, *Behold My Wife!* received decent reviews. Most of the criticism centered the film's last few scenes, where Tonita decides to face punishment for Diana's crime. *Behold My Wife!* tries to deliver a message showing that Tonita is more classy than Michael's family and acquaintances. Audiences, however, have to swallow an uncomfortable amount of slurs and racist jokes.

The cast acted well in the scene's numerous dramatic moments. Raymond especially shined as a hurt man seeking revenge, even though it meant hurting a woman he actually cared about. Owsley and Compton were given plenty of close ups during their scenes, allowing the audience to take in the flawed characters' range of emotions fully. Sidney delivers a lovely performance as Tonita, but the tension between Tonita and Michael might have held more substance with an actual Apache actress.

The effect of the Hays Code is quite noticeable in this film. Though Tonita and Michael are truly in love by the end, they aren't allowed to kiss each other on the mouth a single time during the movie's run. Miscegenation was a "don't" on the list.

It primarily referred to interracial relationships between Black and white people, but it's interesting that Tonita and Michael get to stay married and have a presumable happy ending while also being denied a kiss on screen.

But since kissing was a "be careful" on the list, we also don't get to see Owsley's character lock lips with either Diana or Tonita. Bob has to rely on dialogue alone to woo women. Though some of the lines are delivered quite seductively—"That's your secret. I wanna kiss you and learn them all."—the movie lacks the heated intensity his characters normally brought.

During the winter holidays, Owsley worked on two movies for Paramount simultaneously. He was also seen at a movie premiere with his parents and his date, Virginia Frost. Toward the end of January, he attended a production of the Ziegfeld Follies.

Rumba released in February of 1935. He had a relatively small role in the elaborately staged picture starring George Raft and Carole Lombard. *Rumba* was Raft and Lombard's second picture together after the tremendously successful *Bolero*.

The first part of the movie is set in Havana, Cuba where dancer Joe Martin (Raft) has just won five thousand dollars in a lottery. To his dismay, his winning ticket is counterfeit. Wealthy socialite Diana Harrison (Lombard), however, has the real winning ticket. Joe doesn't hide his anger over this situation, feeling he is more entitled to the money than she. Still, the pair are inexplicably drawn toward each other.

Owsley played Fletcher Hobart, Diana's boyfriend. He's much more conservative than she is and doesn't understand her interest in Cuban music and dancing. When Diana expresses her desires to be lively and human, Fletcher promises to solve her problem by asking her to marry him. She turns him down, though, and becomes enamored with Joe instead.

Cast and crew watching George Raft and Iris Adrian dance while filming Rumba. *Owsley is sitting on the far left side. (courtesy Masheter Movie Archive)*

When Diana's parents request her to come home and marry Fletcher, Diana decides to risk her inheritance and stay with Joe. Joe, however, believes she's going to break up with him, and he plots to beat her to the punch.

Even after getting her heart crushed by Joe, Diana refuses to follow her parents' wishes to marry Fletcher, and Fletcher isn't seen again in the movie. After a publicized threat that Joe might get murdered the next time he performs on stage, the film's sequence of events culminate in a beautiful rumba dance between the characters on stage. Joe and Diana are finally together again.

Reviews for *Rumba* praised the lavish sets and dancing scenes, but the film ultimately failed to capture the same box office success as *Bolero* from the year prior. Much of the sensuality and excitement from *Bolero* is absent in *Rumba,* likely due to the PCA.

Though Owsley's part is minor, he does get into a memorable scrap with Raft's character after Joe makes a move on Diana. Fletcher strikes first, then Joe sends him flying down the stairs. Owsley grabs the stairs' handrail at the last second to prevent hurting himself, but it still must have been a tricky shot.

Owsley's next film, *Goin' to Town,* gave him more scenes, but he was just one of star Mae West's many men. West chose each of her male costars based on how she thought they would appeal to the women in the audience. Owsley "won the role of the good looking, useless society man."[8]

Goin' to Town's set was quite guarded during production, whether at the studio or on location in Pasadena, in order to protect West. Most press weren't allowed to visit the set, and the crew had to be fingerprinted as they left. The fingerprints then had to match in order for the crew to return to the set.[9] West also always had security with her.

West, who wrote the screenplay herself, starred in the movie as Cleo Borden, a saloon dancer. She plans to marry cattleman Buck Gonzales (Fred Kohler), but he's murdered on their wedding day. Still, he's left his entire estate to her—and his land is filled with oil. Instantly, she's a millionaire.

Cleo's enamored by a British land surveyor (Paul Cavanagh) who thinks little of her, and she grabs Edward Carrington's attention by shooting his hat off his head. Her aide Winslow (Gilbert Emery) advises her that she'll need to be of a certain social status in order to win his affections. When she hears that Edward's going to Buenos Aires, she follows him. "I'm going to take a shot at this lady business."

In Buenos Aires, suave gigolo Ivan Valvadov (Ivan Lebedeff) sets his sight on Cleo. Ivan has a mistress (Marjorie Gateson) who dislikes Cleo and feels threatened by the new, young, gorgeous millionaire the society men are fawning over. Brittony

Crane has a nephew named Fletcher Colton (Owsley) who's a heavy gambler and in dire need of money to pay off his debts.

After an exciting horse race at the Palmero track and partying where gambling is a-plenty, Fletcher loses every penny he has. He comes close to taking his own life, but he's stopped by Cleo's aide. Winslow has a proposition for him: marry a rich woman who's seeking his well-established name. Fletcher initially refuses, but he changes his mind after learning the woman in question is Cleo. They agree to marry for business only.

On the night Cleo stages the opera *Samson and Delilah* at her house, she learns that Edward loves her after all. Fletcher shifts from meek to volatile when he learns that Cleo refuses to pay off any more of his gambling debts. He aims to steal money from her, but he's shot during a scuffle with Ivan, who had been hiding in Cleo's room in order to ruin her reputation.

Ivan is uncovered as the murderer after Cleo finds a smoked cigarette with his name on it in her room. Ivan and Brittony both reveal each other's roles in their plot to disgrace Cleo, and the cops take the crooks away. The movie ends with Cleo and Edward, now married to each other, leaving on a trip.

The musical comedy received a fair amount of positive reviews and box office success. West earned the lion's share of the praises with her snappy dialogue, vivid wardrobe, and delightful singing.

Though Owsley had to share his screen time with many others, he performed well, bringing poshness to a character who's swimming in the consequences of his bad choices. He even had the difficult job of spending three days on the floor while they shot the scenes after his character dies.

Tito Coral grabs Ivan Lebedeff while Mae West, in her Delilah outfit, watches. Owsley spent three days on the floor for this scene in Goin' to Town. *(courtesy TCD/Prod.DB)*

Goin' to Town's backdrops are quite memorable, ranging from the busy saloon to the bustling race track. While some of the movie takes place in Buenos Aires, the picture was largely shot in California. To faithfully recreate the famous Palmero race track in Buenos Aires, Cuban newspaperman Francois B. de Valdez supervised the construction of the Argentinian sets.

The movie still holds up superbly, although it's worth noting there are a few racist stereotypes present in some side and minor characters. *Goin' to Town* received a seal of approval from the PCA, a decision which caused some push back from some religious groups for approving of *any* Mae West film.[10] Her reputation for risqué performances had marked her as irrevocably immoral. Too bad they missed a fun film.

As shooting for *Goin' to Town* wrapped up, Owsley appeared in the news for reasons unrelated to his work. He jokingly invited his friends to a party on February 29. 1935 was not a leap year.

A few articles framed him as a hero for saving an actor friend, James Crane, from a fire.[11] While on vacation, Crane started a wood fire in the old-fashioned stove. His flannel pajamas caught fire, and the flames spread. Owsley rushed into the cabin, grabbed a blanket, wrapped it around Crane, and rolled him on the floor to extinguish the flames. They both received burns from the incident.

Soon after that scary event, a humorous article appeared about Owsley attending a tooth-pulling party with Pat O'Brien, Ralph Bellamy, director Mal St. Clair, and agent/manager, Wallace Ross. "They watched their dentist, Dr. Berto Olson, have two teeth taken out."[12]

The spring of 1935 would continue to be quite noteworthy with an unusual, but not entirely unexpected announcement from the car-loving actor.

He had decided to enter a car in the Indianapolis 500.

CHAPTER NINE

Besides tennis, drinking, and playing caddish roles, Monroe Owsley had long been associated with cars and automobile races. He had an interest in all kinds of races—*New Movie* noted Randolph Scott and Monroe Owsley were seen discussing horse race bets at the Santa Anita track that same spring[1]—but he had been driving speedy roadsters since he was young.

On March 23, 1935, Owsley announced he would have a car entered in the Indianapolis 500.[2] He participated in designing the vehicle. The car would be owned by Owsley and two veteran drivers, Harry Hartz and Fred Frame. Auburn Automobile built the Duesenberg with the Miller engine that would be entered. In April, Owsley went to Gilman Hot Springs to do road tests with the car.

The next month, Owsley, Hartz, and Hartz's wife left California to head to Indianapolis. Harris "Harry" Insinger had been named as the driver of their speedster. It was to be his first time driving in the Indianapolis 500 after a remarkable career in California. Hartz declared Insinger was ready for a shot at the hundred thousand dollar prize.

Prior to the Indianapolis 500, Insinger had received numerous injuries in his career, including a broken neck. The "soft-spoken, wild-driving"[3] racer was one of four drivers noted at the time for their action-packed races. Al Gordon, Rex Mays, Kelly Petillo, and Insinger gave California tracks "an air of drama." All four would meet in Speedway that year for the first—and last—time.

For whatever reason, Insinger didn't end up driving for Hartz, Frame, and Owsley on the day of the actual race. He instead drove for the Mikan-Carson team.

Freddie Winnai wound up piloting the Duesenberg. The race started around ten in the morning on May 30 with air aviator Amelia Earhart as that year's honorary referee. Winnai was forced to quit the race on the sixteenth lap due to a broken connecting rod.[4] Petillo would end up roaring to victory that year.

As for Insinger, he ranked fourteenth place, with one hundred and eighty five laps completed. Tragically, he would never get to enter the Indianapolis 500 again. He died in a crash at the Oakland Speedway a few months later.

1935 would prove to be one of the deadliest in Indianapolis 500 history. During his first practice run on May 21, rookie driver Johnny Hannon lost control of his car and ended up having his vehicle land on top of him. He died instantly, and his riding mechanic, Oscar Reeves, was seriously injured. On the same day, Stubby Stubblefield and his mechanic Leo Whitaker died after a crash during the qualifying run.

During the actual race on May 30, Clay Weatherly had insisted on driving Hannon's rebuilt car. He also ended up crashing, perishing near instantly. His riding mechanic, Ed Bradburn, barely survived.

These deaths would result in the formation of the Rookie Orientation Program.

With great disappointment, Owsley left Indiana and returned

to Hollywood. A joke about his drinking appeared in *The New Movie Magazine* that July.[5] Owsley had been sitting in the cocktail lounge of the Hollywood Roosevelt Hotel with his friends, describing a drink he had had long ago. The bartender didn't recognize it, but he tried to recreate it for the actor. While the bartender made the drink, he asked for Owsley's name.

Owsley "swallowed his injured pride" and gave him his name.

"'Ow as in cow,' the bartender said pleasantly. 'All right, we'll name this an Ow Cocktail…after you!'"

Jokes aside, Owsley managed to be a little bit of a real life hero around the same time. A family of five broke down outside of Palm Springs. Owsley spotted the stranded family and took a look at their car. Unable to fix it, he gave the family a ride into town and "then paid the family cash for their wreck."[6]

Owsley spent the rest of that summer filming a picture, although not completely without incident.

Universal's *Remember Last Night?* had a series of perplexing events that left some wondering if the set was haunted. Universal had spent $200,000 erecting an elaborate mansion for the mystery comedy. The press likened this set to a modern day House of Usher.[7]

During production, director James Whale suffered multiple wounds. He received an eye infection, was scalded by boiling tea, and then got knocked down by either a runaway camera or a fallen lamp (or both). He also was injured by a falling large packing box.

Seven additional members of the cast and crew suffered from eye infections. While carrying Constance Cummings, Robert Young fell down an expansive marble staircase and twisted his ankle. An expensive car used for filming lit up into flames mysteriously and was wrecked completely. A car belonging to assistant director Harry Mancke also went up into flames.

Owsley, too, didn't leave the set unscathed. He suffered an

infected foot and had to wear a specially designed shoe. Most of his shots only show him from the calves up.

Remember Last Night? introduces us to an ensemble of rowdy, rich party-goers who are celebrating a married couple's six month marriage anniversary. Young and Cummings played the couple, Tony and Carlotta Milburn. Among the mix of drinkers is a long-suffering, sassy butler named Clarence Phelps, played by Arthur Treacher.

During the long night of partying, tensions rise multiple times between the guests. Vic Huling (George Meeker) doesn't approve of his wife, Bette (Sally Eilers), talking to the Milburns' mechanic, Flannagan (Robert Armstrong), and he suspects her of cheating on him. Owsley's character, Billy Arliss, has romantic designs on the married Penny Whitridge (Louise Henry). Billy also owes money to Vic, who demands he repays his debts immediately. Tony and Vic start to get into a fight, but Jake Whitridge (Reginald Danny) stops them.

The party moves to a restaurant owned by Faronea (Gregory Ratoff). After a cringeworthy moment where most of the guests don blackface masks, the merrymakers start playing with a cannon, outrace the police chasing them, and cause further destruction. Unbeknownst to them, Vic's chauffeur (Jack La Rue's Baptiste Bouclier) is plotting with Faronea to kidnap Vic.

The next morning, the hungover Milburns discover Vic dead in one of their guest rooms, and his wife is missing. Tony calls up a friend, detective Danny Harrison (Edward Arnold). Harrison and his assistant, Maxie (Edward Brophy), leave at once to investigate.

Investigations lead to one conclusion—murder. Vic had been shot through the heart. And not a single guest from the previous night's shenanigans can remember what happened.

While the investigation is underway, Billy and Bette arrive. Bette had spent the night on Billy's porch. She's surprised to hear that Vic has been murdered. A mysterious paper turns up with

Greek writing on it, writing that only Carlotta can decipher. Bette takes poison in an attempt to kill herself, but she's revived by Tony and Carlotta.

Billy's debts become suspect again. He's handcuffed by Danny and taken away for further interrogations inside the house. Carlotta discovers a gun in Tony's night gown and rushes to hide it.

Tony then summons a hypnotist to help recover everyone's memories. The first of the guests to undergo hypnosis, Billy, emerges visibly shaken. After everyone's examined, the hypnotist reveals someone faked their story. Before he can say who, he's shot dead by someone outside.

Tony and Carlotta's investigations lead them to Faronea's restaurant, as he must have been the person to send the Greek note. They overhear Faronea talking to his accomplice, and Faronea ends up dead from a knife to the back. Tony allows Carlotta to get taken by the police so he can pursue Baptiste on his own. But Baptiste is also dead.

As the investigation proceeds, a frightened Billy calls Jake, begging to see him. They agree to meet alone at his house. Billy pleads with him to come alone. "If you double cross me, you won't see me anymore."

When they meet, Billy pulls out a gun. Covered in sweat, Billy is worried the detectives suspect him of murder. He acts out when Tony and Danny arrive, and Jake knocks Billy out cold. Jake then tries to pin everything on Billy, but Billy attempts to shoot Jake. Tony interferes, and Billy winds up dying.

Danny and Tony then solve the case—Billy had been borrowing money from Vic on Jake's behalf. Jake murdered Vic and paid Baptiste to keep quiet, which is why Baptiste killed the hypnotist and Faronea. Jake then killed Baptiste.

With the case solved, Danny makes Tony and Carlotta swear to quit drinking, prompting them to raise a toast to total abstinence. The movie ends with the butler telling everyone off and quitting. They send him off him by throwing food and drinks on him.

Remember Last Night? received mixed reviews from critics. The film's irreverent comedy was decades ahead of its time, down to the namedropping references of Whale's other works, *Bride of Frankenstein* and *Dracula's Daughter.* Though Whale ultimately did not go on to direct *Dracula's Daughter,* he was attached to the project at the time of *Remember Last Night?*'s filming.

Owsley's character is the most suspicious throughout the film, and Owsley delivers a fantastic performance showing the increasing desperation in Billy. Of all the socialites, he's the only one who visibly loses his classy air and turns into a sweaty, pitiful mess. His transformation provides a distinct contrast to Eilers's Bette Huling, who comes out as a woman "born in the gutter and proud of it." Even after her reveal, she maintains a clean visage through the movie without a single hair out of place.

Surprisingly, the film received a seal of approval from the PCA, given how much the plot revolves around excess drinking. The alcohol consumption was tied directly to the film's plot, though, which allowed it to be approved. Whale also skirted censorship with some clever techniques. For example, the picture opens with Tony and Carlotta kissing for nearly thirty seconds, but the camera pans from side to side, so audiences don't see the entire kiss.

As production of *Remember Last Night?* wrapped up, Harrison Carroll reported a gag Owsley had done. "Monroe Owsley doesn't know whether to be complimented or not."[8] He had allegedly donned a bartender's apron and served drinks to a few Hollywood celebrities at the Hollywood Roosevelt Hotel. No one recognized him.

However, a few days later, Carroll reported that Owsley denied it was him. Owsley claimed to be staying away from bars.[9]

The rest of 1935 was quiet for Owsley on the film front. In October, he was briefly linked to Yola d'Avril, and he stayed in Palm Springs for a week in December. As 1936 rolled in, he was spotted at multiple social activities, including a mock bullfight held at Dolores Costello's party. Minna Gombell wore a white mountain goat costume and engaged in "combat" with Helene Costello.[10]

Helene Costello and Owsley made plans to go on tour in March through the Fanchon and Marco agency.[11] The act, written by William E. Barry, would be called *Grease Paint*. Later, there were indications that it would be Sally O'Neil and not Helene Costello to tour with Owsley.

Ultimately, the play didn't happen. While there might have been other reasons the act didn't take off, an important event shook Owsley's life at this time.

His mother passed away.

Some time in 1934, Owsley's parents had moved to Los Angeles to be closer to their son and for Owsley's father's health. Harry M. had retired in 1933 after fifty years in hardware manufacturing, and his health had started to decline. Owsley's sister Gertrude, now a widow, had been staying in Hollywood for the winter.[12] They lived within twenty miles of Owsley's apartment at the time of Gertie's death.

Per her death certificate, Gertie went in for an operation on March 7, 1936 after a sudden onset of intense stomach pain. She had a complete bowel obstruction as well as diverticulitis in her sigmoid colon. During the operation, the surgeon discovered she also had peritonitis, which is an inflammation of the inner wall of the abdomen. Gertie passed away early in the morning on March 13. She was sixty-three.

Harry M.'s health declined further after Gertie's passing. At the time of her death, he was in a hospital for heart troubles. By March of the following year, Owsley's brother and sister-in-law would be living in Santa Monica with Owsley. There's a possibility Gertrude would also join them around that time, but it's difficult to confirm.

Either way, both of the brothers would be close enough to take care of their father.

But it's equally possible the family members were tasked to look after both the senior Owsley and young "Buck." While Owsley denied spending time in bars to the press, there's little doubt he was drinking again.

For now, Owsley's drinking wasn't keeping him from working.

CHAPTER TEN

After a brief mourning period, Monroe Owsley went back to work on a studio lot. Twentieth Century-Fox's *Private Number* began shooting in April of 1936. *Private Number* is a remake of 1930's *Common Clay*, which had been based on the play of the same name by Cleves Kinkead. The remake removed a lot of the original movie's more scandalous elements and added several new characters, resulting in a far different finished product.

Loretta Young, Robert Taylor, and Basil Rathbone starred in *Private Number*. Young played Ellen Neal, a seventeen-year-old girl who takes a job as a servant for the wealthy Winfield family. There, she meets the family's handsome son, Dick (Taylor), who doesn't know she's a servant. Rathbone rounds out the main cast as the film's vile villain. His character, Thomas Wroxton, is the family's persnickety butler and runs the house like a tyrant.

From the moment they meet, Wroxton has eyes on Ellen. She immediately wants to quit because he gives her the creeps, but she's convinced to stay on by another servant, Gracie (Patsy Kelly). While Wroxton makes one of many advances toward Ellen, Gracie whisks her away for a double date.

On the way to the date, she meets a man who returns her lost purse. This suspicious figure is Owsley's James Coakley.

When the double date erupts into a brawl between gangsters and sailors, Gracie meets Coakley again. She also discovers someone has stolen every penny she has from her purse—gee, wonder who did that?

Coakley brings Ellen to meet his grandma at her house. Grandma Gammon (May Beatty) is actually running an illegal gambling parlor. The police happen to raid the parlor that night, and Ellen gets arrested. Since she can't pay her fine, she calls Wroxton to help her.

As the movie proceeds, Ellen furthers her relationship with Dick. They secretly get married, and Ellen is soon pregnant. While Dick's gone, Wroxton discloses both the pregnancy and her previous arrest to the Winfields, and Ellen ends up leaving.

Ellen has her baby alone, and the Winfields try to get the marriage annulled. Dick, however, believes his wife isn't a gold digger—until he sees her in a fancy apartment and confirms she has a police record.

Coakley is brought in to testify during the annulment trial. While Ellen's team had prepared him for their defense, Coakley ends up testifying against her. He blatantly lies, accusing her of taking him to a club and insinuating they had a physical relationship. When the defense attorney (John Miljan) affirms that Ellen was underage on the night in question, he calls for Coakley's arrest.

During a brief recess, Coakley demands to have Wroxton and the prosecutors get him out of the mess. He threatens to tell everyone the truth, and Wroxton reminds him that he already had taken a bribe and that he'd be admitting to committing perjury. Coakley goes to Dick and confesses to everything. Dick punches Wroxton and asks the judge to have the case dismissed. The couple finally reunite in the end.

Basil Rathbone and Robert Taylor in a confrontation after Owsley's confession in Private Number. *Why was the movie called* Private Number? *Still a mystery. ©20th Century Fox (courtesy Everett Collection)*

Private Number generated mixed reviews. It fared better at the box office than its staunchest critics figured it would, thanks to the film's exceptional cast. Young was quite expressive, Taylor oozed charisma, and audiences loved hissing at Rathbone. The romantic drama is quite entertaining for those three actors alone, but Kelly, Miljan, Owsley, the dog who played Hamlet (his name was Prince), and the other side characters gave the film some additional liveliness.

Owsley looks noticeably rough in *Private Number*. The bags under his eyes are dark and heavy. His grief—and likely unhealthy coping methods—couldn't entirely be masked by makeup and studio lights. Still, he turned in a good performance, especially when Coakley fears facing the law for having sex with a minor.

While working on *Private Number*, Owsley joined the cast of

Mr. Cinderella. During filming, Owsley's father visited his son at Hal Roach Studios. Harry met Oliver Hardy, part of comedy team Laurel and Hardy, at the studio and recalled a time back in Atlanta when he would bounce "little Ollie" on his knee.[1]

Mr. Cinderella gave Owsley the chance to remind everyone of his comedic chops. Though the leads, Jack Haley and Betty Furness, have the most screen time, the film's plot centers on Owsley's Aloysius P. Merriweather.

The movie opens with meek, mild-mannered barber Joe Jenkins (Haley) fawning over a socialite featured in a magazine, Patricia Randolph (Furness). Patricia's father (Raymond Walburn) is an automative entrepreneur who needs five million dollars to back his new diesel engine and keep from going bankrupt. He wishes for his daughter to have the wealthy stockholder Aloysius visit them for dinner. Patricia's friend warns her that Aloysius is quite eccentric, but charming. Still, he's prone to wild schemes for a laugh, such as taking a cow to a wedding.

Meanwhile, Joe is struggling to get a hungover Aloysius to wake up and get dressed in his hotel room. "Oh, Joe, drink is a terrible thing. A terrible thing," he says while hugging Joe. Joe then wishes he could be in Aloysius's shoes.

The word "shoes" gives Aloysius an idea. He decides to have Joe go to the Randolphs while pretending to be him, just like Cinderella. Aloysius even proclaims to be Joe's fairy godmother, complete with a wand. "But Cinderella was a girl," Joe protests. Aloysius is undeterred. "All right, so what? You're Mr. Cinderella."

Joe finally gives in and agrees to pose as him, if only to meet Patricia. Before Joe leaves, wearing Aloysius's suit and shoes, the wealthy man offers him a well-intentioned reminder. "If the going gets tough, just telephone your fairy godmother."

Immediately after Joe departs, Aloysius remembers he was supposed to meet his new wife that he's misplaced, Mazie

(Rosina Lawrence). He leaves the hotel and comically gets hit by a car. This accident leads to him being rushed to a hospital without Joe or anyone else knowing of his whereabouts.

At the Randolphs' residence, everyone is pleased to meet the person they think is Aloysius. Patricia and Joe take an immediate liking to each other, but things go haywire, and they wind up spending the night alone on a beach. The next morning, Joe confesses who he really is. Patricia asks him to continue pretending to be Aloysius, fearing her father will go bankrupt without the real Aloysius to back his engine.

Rumors spread when they return. Patricia's Aunt Penelope (Kathleen Lockhart) rushes to announce an engagement. Despite all this, Mr. Randolph continues trying to get money from the man he believes to be Aloysius.

A forlorn Mazie arrives at the hotel Aloysius was supposed to be staying at and discovers he's gone. Her brother (Tom Dugan) has read about the engagement between Aloysius and Patricia in the news. Spike decides to go to the Randolphs and kill Aloysius.

After some further mayhem, the real Aloysius finally wakes up in a hospital. "It's almost midnight," the nurse informs him. He ends up rushing to the Randolphs' residence, where Mazie, Spike, and the police are. Further confusion arises from the mistaken identities, and a chase ensues inside the house.

Eventually, Joe and Aloysius's identities are made clear. To Mr. Randolph's dismay—but Patricia's delight—the real Aloysius bluntly reveals he doesn't have five million dollars. But Joe, however, figures out a way to get the five million dollars needed. The movie ends with a happy ending for everyone but the long-suffering family butler (Arthur Treacher), who agrees to be Joe's best man at his wedding.

"He said he was a good friend of yours." "I am a good friend of his!" "But not that good of a friend!" Owsley, Jack Haley, and Rosina Lawrence in Mr. Cinderella. *(courtesy Everett Collection)*

Mr. Cinderella earned positive reviews for its nonstop laughs and elaborate production values. Director Edward Sedgwick's experience with Buster Keaton's comedies shows in the finished product. The romance between Joe and Patricia also gives the screwball comedy a layer of sweetness, allowing the audience to root for Mr. Cinderella and his Princess Charming.

The entire cast was magnificent in their roles, but Haley and Owsley earn the biggest laughs. Owsley really let himself go in his role to the point it makes sense that *he's* Joe's fairy godmother. Notably, this character actually has a woman who loves him at the end of the movie, although Mazie and Aloysius never get a chance to share a romantic moment on screen.

As production wound up on *Mr. Cinderella,* Owsley stepped away from comedy and joined Universal's *Yellowstone.* Starring

Judith Barrett and Henry Hunter, *Yellowstone* revolves around the mystery of a murdered ex-con and hidden treasure. Barrett played Ruth Foster, a young woman visiting Yellowstone National Park who plans to see her father for the first time. Hunter played Dick Sherwood, a park ranger who's immediately attracted to Ruth.

Ruth's father (Ralph Morgan) is surprised to hear that his daughter is staying at the same inn when he checks into his room. He had been away for eighteen years, allegedly mining in Australia. Their reunion is touching, although it's clear that Jim Foster has some reservations about the situation.

A slew of suspicious men also arrive at the park, including Marty Ryan (Owsley). Ryan is pensive and clearly up to no good. He uses Ruth to get closer to Jim, and he's not too upset when Ruth breaks their date to go to the campfire with Dick. When Jim goes off by himself to his cabin, Ryan follows him.

There, Ryan reveals that he's Tracy Jenkins's son, and he knows that Jim is actually a crook named Anderson. Twenty years prior, Jenkins, Anderson, and a third person named Bald Jack had buried stolen treasure at Yellowstone. Ryan's partner, Dynamite, had worked to spring Jim out of prison in exchange for a fifty-fifty split of the treasure. Now, Ryan wants Jim to recover the money quickly.

Jim soon goes missing. Later, Old Bess erupts for the first time since 1909. The geyser spouts out both boiling hot water and Jim's body. While he had a gunshot wound, he actually died from freezing to death inside the geyser.

An investigation promptly happens, and suspicion falls on Dick due to his ranger's gun having an empty chamber. Ruth follows one of the inn's other guests, Professor Franklin Ross (Rollo Lloyd). He enters a cave located at the bottom of a waterfall. Dick catches up to Ruth and convinces her of his innocence.

The professor uncovers $90,000 of literal cold, hard cash

inside the cave. Ryan follows Franklin inside the cave to confront him. Franklin reveals himself as Bald Jack.

When Ruth and Dick enter the cave, they discover Ryan's dead, having been shot twice. Bald Jack has also frozen to death. The couple manage to escape safely after a confrontation with Jim's real killer.

Owsley and Alan Hale during the murder investigation in Yellowstone. *Paul Fix watches closely. (courtesy Everett Collection)*

Yellowstone received fairly decent reviews. Director Arthur Lubin and his crew incorporated features of Yellowstone National Park into the movie's story. "Of one thing I am most confident, and that is—thanks to the rare beauty of Yellowstone park—we have been able to record one of the most beautiful pictures the screen has known and we are impatient to get it before the public."[2]

Sadly, his promise to deliver gorgeous views of the national park fall quite short. There are very few scenic shots of the natural landscape in the finished product. Most of the film involves interior sets, and the lush potential of the movie's setting is wasted.

Despite this, there are some moments that are visually striking. Glimpses of snow-kissed mountains can be seen occasionally. The massive Old Faithful Inn with its splendid, open lobby is captured in full; it is still the largest log hotel in the world. An actual geyser, most likely Old Faithful, is shown when Old Bess erupts. A lovely waterfall rests against rocky cliffs in such a way that it seems like a painting.

Lubin had some good shots for the cast too. While Old Bess erupts, each living character's face is shown, and they all tell a different story. Ryan's reveal as Tracy Jenkins's son has added tension thanks to the way the fireplace enhances Owsley's signature sneer.

The script didn't call for either Barrett or Hunter to do much to demonstrate their acting capabilities, unfortunately. The best performances were given by Morgan, Owsley, and Alan Hale. Andy Devine and Raymond Hatton did quite well as the film's comic reliefs.

A news article circulated that Paul Fix had finally broken his death streak in *Yellowstone*.[3] Supposedly, Fix's Dynamite character was his first character in five years not to die on screen. While this might not be one hundred percent true, it makes for a good laugh. Owsley, who also frequently dies in his movies, probably could have commiserated with Fix.

Immediately after *Yellowstone*'s release, Owsley found himself back at Paramount. In *Hideaway Girl,* he gave his last performance as a truly villainous cad. Shirley Ross played Toni Ainsworth, who almost marries a phony count named Count de Montaigne and regrets it. It's not hard to guess that Owsley played the count.

Toni escapes from the count and takes his car in the process. She finds refuge on a yacht owned by the dashing Mike Winslow (Robert Cummings) and tells him her name is Belinda. The police, who are pursuing Toni because they think she's a jewel thief, believe Mike and "Belinda" are a married couple. This causes problems for the very much engaged Mike.

As Mike and Toni fall in love, Count de Montaigne is revealed to be a crook named Jake. Jake recognizes Mike's fiancée (Wilma Francis) as the jewel thief, Lady Jane. Jake and Lady Jane get arrested, and Mike and Toni have their happily ever after.

Owsley, Robert Cummings, and Shirley Ross figuring things out in Hideaway Girl. *(courtesy Everett Collection)*

Hideaway Girl relied on a lot of comedy and songs to tie the more thrilling elements together. The film earned a fair amount of praise, though the actress Martha Raye seemed to divide critics. They either loved her, or they really couldn't stand her. As her character isn't central to the main romance, it's understandable if her scenes disrupted the flow of the movie.

Hollywood Spectator had praise for Owsley in their review that otherwise tore down Raye's presence. They wrote Owsley gave "a smoothly finished characterization of a sophisticated crook."[4] *The Kansas City Star* had less impressive words for him, summing up their review of him to "he is an easily acceptable villain."[5]

After *Hideaway Girl* finished production, Owsley took it easy for the rest of the year—or perhaps he lost himself in his vices trying to overcome the anguish inside him.

As the next chapter will make clear, the end had long started for the tormented actor.

CHAPTER ELEVEN

In the summer and early fall of 1936, Monroe Owsley was linked to multiple women. Sally Rand, Mary McCormic, and Helen Twelvetrees were among the beautiful women he was seen dancing with and escorting about town. As late fall settled in, Owsley had a Navy officer as a frequent house guest. Unnamed women were rumored to follow whenever Herschel House stayed with him.[1]

Owsley invited House to go golfing with him one day in December. Along the way, Owsley asked, "Mind if I take my girl along?" He stopped at Anita Page's place and came back out with the actress.

Page and House were instantly smitten with each other. "I guess it must have been love at first sight with both of us, for I remember that I just walked around the golf course in a daze," Page confided in a 1947 interview.[2] House told friends that he proposed to her on the tenth hole.

The couple eloped nineteen days later on January 8, 1937. Owsley was unhappy about it all, and he even begged Page not to marry House. When she decided to go through with it, Owsley told her, "Well, if he ever mistreats you, you let me know."[3]

Page and House stayed married until the latter's death in 1991.

Owsley joined Republic Pictures for *The Hit Parade* in February that year. *The Hit Parade* would be his last film.

Louise Henry getting rid of Phil Regan and replacing him with Owsley in The Hit Parade. *Harvey Clark and Kathleen Howard observe nearby. (courtesy Everett Collection)*

Frances Langford and Phil Regan starred in the musical comedy that hosted a huge roster of talents, including Duke Ellington and his orchestra. The plot is rather thin so as to allow the musical and comedy acts to have their turn in the spotlight, but there is a story to follow.

Pete Garland (Regan) is a poor agent for wealthy singer Monica Barrett (Louise Henry) and also in love with her. Monica betrays Pete when she tosses him aside for the high class lawyer, Teddy Leeds (Owsley). After knocking out Teddy, Pete begins his search for a new singer to raise to stardom.

His search ends when he hears Ruth Allison (Langford) sing. Immediately, Pete wants to sign with her. Unbeknownst to him, Ruth is an ex-convict who has jumped parole and is being pursued by a parole officer.

After much work, Ruth starts rising in popularity, and she begins to develop feelings for Pete. Pete, however, is still hung up on Monica. Meanwhile, Monica is pushed and verbally abused by the man running the radio show she's on for not singing popular songs. She quits the show, and Ruth takes her place.

In a fit of jealousy, Monica exposes Ruth's convict past to the press. Ruth goes into hiding, which prompts Pete to organize a broadcast pleading for her return. When Ruth finally comes back, her parole officer shows up and gives her a pardon from the governor. Pete and Ruth end the movie with a kiss.

The Hit Parade earned fairly positive reviews from critics, although a modern watch of the movie doesn't inspire the same amount of praise. While there were wonderful performances from Langford, Regan, Max Terhune, Ivie Anderson, Duke Ellington and his orchestra, and many others, the film has several confusing parts.

Some of this confusion could be attributed to Republic trimming eighteen minutes from the picture and renaming it to *I'll Reach for a Star*. This version is the most widely seen one today. Unfortunately, the shorter version of *The Hit Parade* still has a blatantly racist blackface skit from Pat Padgett and Pick Malone.

Owsley's role was small in this picture, but it was quite interesting. He's supposed to play an antagonist, however, it's hard to think of him as a bad guy. Snooty, yes, but not bad. His character is loyal to Monica to the very end. He keeps her best interests at heart, even in her declining popularity.

The brief fight between Pete and Teddy is almost unsettling when one considers how *The Hit Parade* was Owsley's last film. After Pete knocks out Teddy, Pete throws a bouquet of flowers on top of him. "Rest in peace, sweetheart," he says to Teddy. Owsley had gone through numerous physical altercations and deaths in his various roles, but no character had ever so blatantly to told his character to rest in peace.

Owsley would be dead within weeks after the movie's release.

Owsley stopped appearing in gossip columns for the most part during the first half of 1937. He would be linked to Claire Windsor and seen at the occasional social event, but mentions of his personal life were seldom. He had no other movies lined up immediately after finishing *The Hit Parade*.

Owsley pictured with his father in the January 1936 issue of Cine-Mundial. *(courtesy Media History Digital Library)*

A dark shadow fell over Owsley's life on May 5 when his father passed away. Harry M. was a week shy of his seventy-sixth birthday. He was buried beside his wife at Forest Lawn Memorial Park.[4]

Harry M.'s cause of death was listed in his death certificate as cerebral thrombosis and myocardial degeneration. Generalized artery sclerosis, old coronary thrombosis, and seniority were named as contributors. Some of the terms are dated in today's world of medicine, but he had heart failure and a blood clot in his brain that led to his death.

As Owsley settled affairs with his father's passing, he updated his own will on May 20. Then he traveled to San Francisco.

The Golden Gate Bridge had just finished being built, and there were big festivities planned for the bridge's opening. The Fiesta started on May 27 with Pedestrian Day, and the second day allowed automobiles to cross the bridge. Owsley continued the party in Del Monte, then he went to stay with an "old friend" in San Mateo.[5]

This friend was listed as George Nichols in some articles. Nichols was possibly Owsley's sister-in-law's brother, as Katherine had family in San Mateo and a brother named George. If not her brother, the person could have been her brother's son or one of her other siblings' sons.

Redwood City Tribune reported that Owsley was "stricken" while in San Mateo. Late at night on either June 4 or 5, Dr. Rebec was called to Nichols's house. The doctor saw Owsley was in critical condition and had him rushed to Twin Pines sanitarium.[6]

On June 7, 1937, Monroe Righter "Buck" Owsley passed at 8:30 A.M. He was thirty-six years old.

His heart had taken too much damage from his heavy drinking. The principal cause of death listed on his death certificate was chronic myocarditis with acute alcoholism as a contributory cause. Today, the term would most likely be alcoholic cardiomyopathy or alcohol-induced cardiomyopathy.

His brother requested no publicity while making arrangements for Owsley's body.[7] Harry Albert said he would make a statement to the press later. He then accompanied his brother's remains back to Los Angeles. A cousin drove Owsley's Duesenberg from San Mateo.

The story Harry Albert and Owsley's agent, Dick Polimer, gave to the press was that Owsley had passed away from a heart attack caused by acute indigestion.[8] Details were kept to a minimum, and many articles reported conflicting details, such as where he had died.

Owsley was buried beside his parents at Forest Lawn Memorial Park on June 9. Hours earlier, Jean Harlow's funeral had been held at the same cemetery. Dozens of floral wreaths covered the silver metal coffin. Around one hundred people attended his funeral, including Harry Albert and Gertrude. Hollywood Methodist Church pastor Reverend G.R. Phillips officiated—he had led the services for both of Owsley's parents. The service concluded with the organ playing Owsley's favorite melody, "Boots and Saddles."[9]

Nearly three weeks later, Owsley's will was probated. No value other than "in excess of $10,000" was named, but an imaginary wife being included in the will generated buzz in newspapers.

"To my wife, if she be living with me at the time of my death, all my moneys, stock and jewelry, my automobile and household effects."[10]

The will further stipulated that should his wife remarry within three years of his death, the estate should go back to executors and be redistributed as though she had never existed.

If Owsley had someone in mind when he wrote the will is a mystery. As there was no such wife, sixty percent of his estate went to his cousin, Charles O. Dixon. Thirty-five percent went to Harry Albert, and the remaining five percent went to Gertrude. Owsley explained in his will that Dixon had more need for inheritance than his siblings.

With Jean Harlow's death overshadowing Owsley's death, there were few write ups about the actor after his passing. Cameron Shipp of *The Charlotte News* noted that Owsley, being too good of a newspaperman, wouldn't have missed the irony about being unable to make front page news against Harlow. Shipp briefly reflected on his friendship with Owsley, recalling the way the pair would talk about athletes like Albie Booth and Bitsy Grant.[11]

Owsley's name continued to appear in newspapers that summer, often linked with Harlow's and other notable Hollywood people who died prematurely, due to the superstition that death comes in threes. Comedy writer Al Boasberg died from a heart attack on June 18. Colin Clive, another actor with alcohol issues, passed away on June 25 from complications of tuberculosis.

As the months went on and Owsley's movies gradually began to leave theaters, his name faded from the public memory. There were a few mentions of him when *Holiday* was remade with Katharine Hepburn as the lead—Lew Ayres took over Owsley's role. Louis Sobol recalled in 1947 how Owsley had had a part in one of Sobol's plays, but he quit after three days. "It stinks. I'd rather shovel snow."[12]

In time, Owsley became forgotten. Almost none of his fellow actors or actresses talked about him in their memoirs decades later. Anita Page, who wound up being one of the last surviving Hollywood silent film stars, spoke of Owsley occasionally when she talked about meeting her husband. She passed away in 2008 at the age of ninety-eight.

Harry Albert joined his brother and parents in death on July 7, 1952 at the age of sixty-eight. His wife, Katherine, outlived him by almost thirty years, meeting her end in 1980. Gertrude spent the last twenty years of her life in Santa Monica and passed at the age of seventy-seven on November 25, 1958. Both Harry Albert and Gertrude are buried with their parents and "Buck" at Forest Lawn Memorial Park. Neither of them were survived by any children.

For over fifteen years, Monroe Owsley devoted himself to his career and dreams. He spoke openly about the bitter relationship he had with Hollywood. He struggled to find happiness on screen and away from the cameras. He worked with legends like Gloria Swanson, Joan Crawford, and Bette Davis, but his name is unknown to the majority of classic cinema fans.

Still, his legacy survives in his filmography. He hated playing cads, but he did the job well. Watching him is never boring.

When considering Owsley's life as a whole, it's hard not to think of his performance during the end of *Holiday*, when Ned gives a toast to Linda. He's stuck in a miserable place, but he's hopeful that he'll get out one day. The scene perfectly reflects Owsley's attitude toward his career and possibly other aspects of his complicated life.

Owsley giving at toast at the end of Holiday. *(from author's personal collection)*

The next time you have a drink, with or without alcohol, raise a toast to the Ace of Cads.

AFTERWORD

This section will address some rumors and speculations about Monroe Owsley. The analysis is based off this particular author's extensive research. Readers are encouraged to draw their own conclusions.

Currently, the Internet is awash with misinformation about how Owsley died. Most of this is due in part to his brother's decision to hide the true nature of Owsley's death. Why Harry Albert decided to do that is still a mystery, but it's easy to make assumptions. Alcohol use disorders and mental illnesses still carry heavy stigmas in 2024. Harry Albert likely wanted to protect his family from scandal and protect his brother's legacy.

Unfortunately, he might have succeeded too well in controlling the narrative. If the truth had been revealed, Owsley might have stayed in the public's perception for far longer than he actually did. If nothing else, the truth could have prompted much needed public discussions about excessive alcohol and substance use.

While it's possible Harry Albert was pressured by outside forces, such as film studios, to keep the alcohol use part of

Owsley's death a secret, it seems doubtful. Old Hollywood studios certainly have a reputation for covering up sensational deaths, even though the allegations often have little evidence to support them.

One prominent example is the case of Paul Bern, Jean Harlow's second husband. A few MGM executives claimed that they were notified of Bern's apparent suicide before the police were told. Studio head Louis B. Mayer allegedly figured that pinning Bern's suicide on his impotence would best protect Harlow from a career-destroying scandal. Samuel Marx and Henry Hathaway believed that Bern had been murdered by his common law wife, who killed herself shortly after. These claims came years after both Harlow and Mayer's deaths.

Often in cases of studio cover up rumors, the star is a major financial asset to the studios. Owsley was not working on any movies at the time of his death, nor did he seem to have a contract with any studio. The impact and size of his roles had started dwindling significantly in the Hays Code era of Hollywood. Plus, he had been a freelancer for several years. No studio would have felt the need to cover up his death.

Rumors about Owsley's death rippled into wild claims over the decades. Some newspapers began to confuse the details of Owsley's death in the late 1930s, attributing his demise to a car accident. The car accident detail lingers on some websites today. Ray Milland wrote in his memoir that a horse killed Owsley.

Owsley's death certificate does not name any external injuries as contributing factors to his end. There are also no contemporaneous reports about Owsley being in a car or riding accident. It's hard to imagine an accident would have gone unwritten by local journalists.

Curiously, Ralf Harolde—who also had a reputation for playing villainous roles on screen—sometimes appears in rumors about Owsley. There are claims he was involved in the car accident that killed Owsley, and some sites claim they were romantically involved with each other.

As far as the first half of the rumor goes, there's no credible evidence that Harolde had anything to do with Owsley's death. The story might have spun from someone mixing up the fact that Harolde *had* killed an employee theater named Harry Gilbert in a car accident. The incident occurred in 1928, nine years before Owsley's death.

Harolde disappeared from the limelight for about two years shortly after Owsley's death, but he had gotten involved in a very different scandal. In 1938, he was arrested on suspicion for kidnapping and loitering on a public school grounds. He had taken a little boy to buy ice cream, and he claimed to have had no ulterior motive. The boy's mother eventually forgave Harolde.

Was Harolde involved in Owsley's death? Most unlikely. Were Harolde and Owsley ever lovers? It's not improbable, but there's currently no concrete evidence for it.

Owsley's romantic life is still quite mysterious. Lawrence J. Quirk noted in *Fasten Your Seat Belts* that Owsley had rumors about "homosexual seductions which he conducted with the utmost intensity" as well as reports of scandals involving drug use, alcohol, and gambling.

Quirk passed in 2014, but I reached out to Quirk's partner and frequent collaborator, William Schoell, to see if he knew of anything related to Monroe Owsley. He kindly responded that he didn't know and humorously noted that Quirk kept most of his research inside his head.

Still, Quirk's claims in *Fasten Your Seat Belts* shouldn't be entirely overlooked. Quirk was the nephew of James R. Quirk, an editor and publisher for *Photoplay* magazine. He took after his uncle and wrote about celebrities. Over his lengthy career, Quirk wrote dozens of books about movie stars and spoke with many screen legends directly.

It's already been established that Owsley had alcohol issues and engaged in gambling, and it's not farfetched to imagine he had used other substances. It's equally not unbelievable that Owsley might have been gay, bisexual, or something other than heterosexual.

Multiple times through his career, Owsley complained about not getting a woman on stage or on screen. He also asserted his desire to marry in real life several times, but he never did. Any time he was engaged, it was quickly denied or broken. The engagements almost seemed like publicity stunts more than actual romantic entanglements gone awry.

Before his nervous breakdown, Hollywood gossips never wrote about him with women. *Motion Picture* magazine even noted in May of 1931 that they hadn't been able to scent out a romance. It was only after his comeback in 1932 that he was seen with women in public. Rarely the same woman was named more than once in gossip columns.

If Owsley was queer, it's possible his career was affected as the Hays Code became enforced. While queer people were still not quite accepted in the early days of Hollywood, numerous people in the movie industry were open about their sexualities. Tightened censorship in the early 1930s forced many "out" folks to hide their sexualities. Famously, screen heartthrob William Haines refused to go back into the closet, and he quit acting in 1934.

The rumors of Owsley's homosexual seductions might have made studio executives reluctant to give him the same large roles he had had earlier in his career. It's equally possible Owsley's drinking—and other vices—kept him from furthering his career. Or maybe the answer lies within some combination of all of the above.

The repeal of the Prohibition Act and the formation of the PCA happened in the same time span as the noticeable decline of Owsley's roles. Alcohol was seen in a more favorable light on screen, and it had become less difficult to produce, sell, import, and transport alcohol. The rising availability of alcohol plus increasing stress probably made it easier for Owsley to give in to his compulsions. Excessive drinking can lead to people being difficult to work with or outright unavailable.

His drinking wasn't a moral failure on his part. Alcohol use disorder is a serious medical and mental condition. Even with all the support and care in the world, some people are unable to manage their alcohol dependency.

Owsley's alcohol use definitely affected his life. It probably affected his career too. Maybe it also interfered with his romantic intentions, whatever those might have been.

There's a lot about Monroe Owsley that fans still don't know. Putting together this book meant getting three new questions every time I answered one. I'm hopeful this book might prompt some people who have answers to come forward, but it's quite likely some questions will never be answered.

Who was Monroe Owsley? He was a handsome, talented actor with troubles and a condition that magnified those troubles. He left us plenty of examples of his works to enjoy, but he also left us too soon. That much I can answer confidently.

Who was he, really? I don't know. I can only guess.

So long as I live, I won't stop asking.

Easter on the Desert—by Katherine Nichols Owsley

They say that you are wild and desolate,
You, who sweep the West with sandy dunes,
You, who live, devouring space, with naught
For little things; Eating the land that spreads
The miles to every rock-hewn eminence.

You are wild and desolate! You,
Who nurse the new-born flowers upon your breast:
Verbenas, purple, pink, and red as fire,
And poppies yellower than yellow suns
That hide behind horizons when you sleep.
White lilies, pure and humble as the Christ
Who died upon the Cross, lift waxen heads
Above thorned stems (For now, no head is thorned,
Only heavy hearts are pricked and bleed
That beat behind silk gowns and clean starched shirts.)
Yuccas, the tall candle flowers that light
The night with bloom, and red-tipped ocatillas
That point their spiny fingers to the sky,
Call the Spring that ushers Easter in.

They say that you are wild and desolate,
You, who bring to birth the fragrant blooms
No city knows....Wild and desolate!
You, who wear a rainbow on your breast!

TIMELINE FOR MONROE OWSLEY'S IMMEDIATE FAMILY

May 12, 1861: Harry Monroe Owsley is born; parents are Asher Bodine and Susan G. Colley Owsley

August 4, 1872: Gertrude "Gertie" Alice Righter is born; parents are Dr. Charles and Abigail Righter

June 2, 1879: Abigail J. "Abbie" Righter passes away from illness

October 19, 1880: Harry M. Owsley and Ida Matthews marry

July 18, 1881: Gertrude McVeigh Owsley is born; parents are Harry M. and Ida Owsley

July 11, 1883: Harry Albert Owsley is born; parents are Harry M. and Ida Owsley

August 20, 1891: Asher Bodine Owsley passes away from illness

1892: Ida Owsley passes away

December 13, 1893: Harry M. Owsley and Gertie Righter marry

August 11, 1900: Monroe Righter Owsley is born; parents are Harry M. And Gertie Owsley

June 12, 1902: Gertrude Owsley and A. Scott Ledbetter marry

1903: John Scott Ledbetter is born; parents are Gertrude and A. Scott Ledbetter

1903-1906: A. Scott Ledbetter leaves Gertrude Owsley at some point and marries another woman by 1906

February 5, 1903: Abbie Letella Owsley is born; parents are Harry M. and Gertie Owsley

March 18, 1903: Dr. Charles C. Righter passes away from illness

July 19, 1903: Abbie Letella Owsley passes away from illness

October 24, 1909: Susan G. Colley Owsley passes away from illness

July 7, 1918: Harry Albert Owsley and Katherine Nichols marry

November 9, 1919: John Ledbetter and friend Raymond Iszard die from either drowning or exposure during duck hunting trip

May 12, 1922: Gertrude Owsley marries David LeGrande Hedges, general manager of *Good Housekeeping* magazine

October 11, 1933: David LeGrande Hedges passes away from illness

March 13, 1936: Gertie Owsley passes away from illness

May 5, 1937: Harry M. Owsley passes away from illness

June 7, 1937: Monroe Owsley passes away from illness

July 7, 1952: Harry Albert Owsley passes away from illness

November 25, 1958: Gertrude Owsley Hedges passes away from illness

July 14, 1980: Katherine Nichols Owsley passes away

STAGE PRODUCTIONS

Plays performed around 1922-1923.

* *The Importance of Being Earnest* by Oscar Wilde

Cast: Charles Callahan, Sterling Holloway, Spencer Tracy, Ellsworth Jones, Monroe Owsley, June Webster, Barbara Wilson, Dorothy Hodgens, Suzanne Powers

* *The Marrying of Ann Leete* by Harley Granville-Barker
* *The Charlatan* by Leonard Praskins and Ernest Pascal
* *Three Live Ghosts* by Frederic S. Isham
* *The Thirteenth Chair* by Bayard Veller

On the Redpath Chautauqua circuit; summer 1923.

* *The Meanest Man in the World* by Augustin MacHugh, based on a skit by Everett Ruskay

Cast: George Westlake, Marion Evensen, William Friend, Monroe Owsley, Charles Seele, Jean Neilson, Clem Bevans, Louis Frohoff

Traveling production of *Merton of the Movies*; October 1923-April 1924.

* *Merton of the Movies* by Marc Connolly and George S. Kaufman, based on the novel *Merton of the Movies* by Harry Leon Wilson

Cast: Edward M. Favor, Bert Melville, Glenn Hunter, Helen Royton, Franchon Campbell, J.K. Murray, Albert Cowles, Wilton Lackaye, Jr., Joseph Lothian, Jean Ford, Romaine Callender, Tom Hadaway, John Webster, Alexander Clark, Jr., Dorothy Heath, Ruth Mitchell, Monroe Owsley, Edith Janney, William Adler, Billy Janney, M.A. Buser, A.L. Ehrman

Notes: Owsley doubled for Glenn Hunter

August 1924 and October 1924.

* *Spring and the Moonlight* by Edwin Burke

Cast: Fritzi Brunette, Robert Daly, Monroe Owsley, and Warren Ashe

With The Dramatists' Theater, Inc.; September and October 1924.

* *The Goose Hangs High* by Lewis Beach

Director: James Forbes

Stage setting: Livingston Platt

Cast: George Alison, Lorna Elliott, Julia Stuart, Guy Standing, Jr., Monroe Owsley, Kathleen Middleton, Patricia Morris, Dallas Tyler, Geoffrey Wardwell, Bernard Craney, Frederick Smith, Forrest Cummings, Berenice Parker, Berry Middleton

With the Stuart Walker Company. George Somnes as director, Charles Elrod as the art director. Spring and summer 1925.

* *The Best People* by Avery Hopwood and David Gray; week of April 13.

Cast: Ralph Kellard, Leonore Sorsby, Monroe Owsley, Betsy Jane Southgate, Corbet Morris, George Alison, Teresa Dale, William Evarts, Lucile Nikolas, and Regina Stanfiel

* *Little Old New York* by Rida Johnson Young; week of April 20.

Cast: Ralph Kellard, Corbet Morris, James Barton, William Evarts, Ralph Urmy, L'Estrange Millman, Helen Baysinger, Jack King Davis, Teresa Dale, Monroe Owsley, Francis Murray, Lucile Nikolas, Leonore Sorsby, Francis Murray, Clark Keeney

* *The Goose Hangs High* by Lewis Beach; week of April 27.

Cast: George Alison, Teresa Dale, Corbet Morris, L'Estrange Millman, Regina Stanfiel, Leonore Sorsby, Eugenia Curtis as Mrs. Bradley, Ralph Kellard, Ralph Urmy, Lucile Nikolas, Monroe Owsley, Helen Baysinger, William Evarts, Francis Murray

* *Chicken Feed* by Guy Bolton; week of May 11.

Cast: George Alison, Teresa Dale, Eugenia Curtis, William Evarts, Ralph Kellard, Lucile Nikolas, Monroe Owsley, Francis Murray, Alan Foud, Ray Nasser, Regina Stanfiel

* *In the Next Room* by Eleanor Robson and Harriet Ford, adapted from *The Mystery of the Boule Cabinet* by Burton E. Stevenson; week of May 18.

Cast: Ralph Kellard, Lucile Nikolas, Monroe Owsley, Eugenia Curtis, George Alison, William Evarts, Teresa Dale, Helen Baysinger, Jack King Davis, Alan Foud

* *The Best People* by Avery Hopwood and David Gray; week of May 25.

Cast: Ruth Hammond, George Alison, Leonore Sorsby, William Evarts, Corbett Morris, Ralph Kellard, Monroe Owsley, Teresa Dale, Betsy Jane Southgate, Regina Stanfiel, Ralph Urmy, John Storey

* *Kiki* by David Belasco, adapted from the book by André Picard; week of June 1.

Cast: Lucile Nikolas, Ralph Kellard, Leonore Sorsby, Mona Burns, George Alison, William Evarts, Monroe Owsley, Eugenia Curtis, Regina Stanfiel, Helen Baysinger, Raymond Nasser, Margaret Myers

* *Meet the Wife* by Lynn Starling; week of June 8.

Cast: Spring Byington, Aldrich Bowker, Lucile Nikolas, L'Estrange Millman, Monroe Owsley, Corbet Morris, Rikel Kent

* *Just Married* by Adelaide Matthews and Anne Nichols; week of June 15.

Cast: Monroe Owsley, Regina Stanfiel, Ray Nassur, Marjorie MacLucas, Alan Foud, William Evarts, Eugenia Curtis, Francis Murray, Mona Bruns, Larry Fletcher, L'Estrange Millman, Ralph Kellard, Lucile Nikolas, Ralph Urmy

* *Smilin' Through* by Allan Langdon (Jane Cowl and Jane Murfin); week of June 22.

Cast: Lucile Nikolas, Ralph Kellard, Larry Fletcher, Monroe Owls, L'Estrange Millman, Mona Bruns, Regina Stanfiel, Helen Baysinger, Ralph Urmy

* *Grounds for Divorce* by Guy Bolton, adapted from Ernest Vadja's original play; week of June 29.

Cast: Lucile Nikolas, Ralph Kellard, L'Estrange Millman, Corbet Morris, Teresa Dale, Marjorie MacLucas, Monroe Owsley, Regina Stanfiel, Helen Baysinger, William Evarts

* *Clarence* by Booth Tarkington; week of July 6.

Cast: Ralph Kellard, Leonore Sorsby, Teresa Dale, Monroe Owsley, William Evarts, Betsy Jane Southgate, Rikel Kent, Marjorie MacLucas, Regina Stanfiel, Helen Baysinger

With The Dramatists' Theater, Inc.; November 1925-March 1926.

* *Young Blood* by James Forbes

Director: James Forbes

Set director: Clark Robinson

Cast: Norman Trevor, Eric Dressler, Florence Eldridge, Monroe Owsley, Helen Hayes, Malcolm Duncan, Cameron Clemens

With the The Poli Players. Arthur Holman as director. Spring and summer 1926.

* *Easy Come, Easy Go* by Owen Davis; week of April 26.

Cast: Leonard Lord, Harry Fischer, Frank Camp, Arthur Holman, Walter Horton, Bertram Perry, Monroe Owsley, Sidney Mansfield, Rita Coakley, Elizabeth Duray, Virginia Lee Moore, Edyth Ketchum

* *The Family Upstairs* by Harry Delf; week of May 3.

Cast: Walter Horton, Edyth Ketchum, Rita Coakley, Monroe Owsley, Elizabeth Duray, Leonard Lord, Virginia Lee Moore, Harry Fisher

* *Silence* by Max Marcin; week of May 10.

Cast: Monroe Owsley, Sidney Mansfield, Frank Camp, Walter Horton, John Taylor, Edyth Ketchum, Harry Fischer, Elizabeth Duray, Arthur Holman, Rita Coakley, Thomas V. Morrison, Leonard Lord, Virginia Lee Moore

* *The Song and Dance Man* by George M. Cohan; week of May 17.

Cast: Foster Williams, Eve Nansen, Frank Camp, Edyth Ketch, Harry Fischer, Arthur Holman, Elizabeth Duray, Virginia Lee Moore, Monroe Owsley, Sidney Mansfield

* *Kiki* by David Belasco, adapted from the book by André Picard; week of May 24.

Cast: Foster Williams, Frank Camp, Walter Horton, Monroe Owsley, Arthur Holman, Harry Fischer, Sidney Mansfield, Virginia Lee Moore, Elizabeth Duray, Mary Thorp, Vivian Barry, Helen Horne, Huldy Mason, Edyth Ketchum, Eve Nansen

* *Irene* by James Montgomery. Lyrics by Joseph McCarthy. Score by Harry Tierney. Week of May 31.

Cast: Foster Williams, Monroe Owsley, Frank Camp, Harry Fischer, Walter Horton, Eve Nansen, Elizabeth Duray, Helen Landis, Virginia Lee Moore, Vivian Barry, Edyth Ketchum, Beatrice Howarth, Busby Berkeley

* *The Poor Nut* by J.C. and Elliott Nugent; week of June 7.

Cast: Sidney Mansfield, Eve Nansen, Virginia Lee Moore, Foster Williams, Harry Fischer, Busby Berkeley, Frank Camp, Monroe Owsley, Walter Horton, Arthur Holman, Arthur Griffen, George M. Cavanaugh, Elizabeth Duray, Edyth Ketchum, Helen Horne

* *Dear Me* by Luther Reed and Hale Hamilton; week of June 14.

Cast: Eve Nansen, Foster Williams, Sidney Mansfield, Harry Fischer, Arthur Holman, Monroe Owsley, Elizabeth Duray, Walter Horton, Frank Camp, Edyth Ketchum

* *Love 'Em and Leave 'Em* by George Abbott and John V. A. Weaver; week of June 21.

Cast: Alice Baxter, Frank Camp, Harry Fischer, Monroe Owsley, Foster Williams, Elizabeth Duray, Eve Nansen, Edyth Ketchum, Walter Horton, Sidney Mansfield

* *Mrs. Murphy in Society* by Gracie Emmett; week of June 28.

Cast: Harry Fischer, Monroe Owsley, Elizabeth Duray, Gracie Emmett, Sidney Mansfield, Arthur Holman, Edyth Ketchum, Eve Nansen, Rita Jones, Foster Williams, Alice Baxter, Frank Camp, Walter Horton

* *The Gorilla* by Ralph Spence; week of July 5.

Cast: Busby Berkeley, Walter Horton, Eve Nansen, Foster Williams, Frank Camp, Harry Fischer, Monroe Owsley, Walter Donahue, Arthur Holman, William Harvey, Sidney Mansfield

* *Molly Darling* by Otto Harbach and William Carey Duncan. Lyrics by Phil Cook. Score by Tom Johnstone. Week of July 12 (Owsley filled in the night of July 12 only).

Cast: Monroe Owsley, Frank Camp, Elizabeth Duray, Busby Berkeley, Bessie Gross, Walter Horton, Sidney Mansfield

Traveling production of *The Great Gatsby*. Produced by William A. Brady. August 1926-November 1926.

* *The Great Gatsby* by Owen Davis, adapted from the book by F. Scott Fitzgerald

Cast: Monroe Owsley, Elsa Gray, James Rennie, Charles Dickson, William Meehan, John Clubley, Helen Baxter, Walter Davis, Catherine Willard, Josephine Evans, Ray Birdwell, Richard Rawson, Ruth Day, Edna Jones, Caroline Swift, William Crimans, Pascal Cowan, Elsa Gray, Giuseppe Caruso

April-May 1927.

* *Night Hawk* by Roland Oliver

Cast: Donnee Waldron, Belle D'Arcy, William Courtenay, Monroe Owsley, Isabelle Lowe

November 1928-November 1929.

* *Holiday* by Philip Barry. Produced by Arthur Hopkins.

Cast: Hope Williams, Ben Smith, Dorothy Tree, Monroe Owsley, Barbara White, Donald Ogden Stewart, Walter Walker, Rosalie Norman, Thaddeus Clancy, J. Ascher Smith, Cameron Clemens, Beatrice Ames

FILMOGRAPHY

* *Jim the Penman*

Release date: April 1921

Director: Kenneth Webb

Writers: Dorothy Farm; based on the original play *Jim the Penman* by Charles Lawrence Young

Cinematography: Tom L. Griffith, Harry Stradling

Cast: Lionel Barrymore, Ned Burton, Charles Coghlan, James Laffey, Gladys Leslie, Douglas MacPherson, Anders Randolf, Arthur Rankin, Doris Rankin, Monroe Owsley

Notes: Owsley's role is unconfirmed. *Jim the Penman* is missing one reel.

* *The First Kiss*

Release date: August 1928

Director: Rowland V. Lee

Writers: John Farrow and Tom Reed; based on *Four Brothers* by Tristram Tupper

Cinematography: Alfred Gilks

Production company: Paramount Pictures

Cast: Fay Wray, Gary Cooper, Lane Chandler, Leslie Fenton, Paul Fix, Malcolm Williams, Monroe Owsley

Notes: Considered to be a lost film.

* *Carry On, Sergeant!*

Release date: November 1928

Director: Bruce Bairnsfather

Writer: Bruce Bairnsfather

Cinematography: Bert Cann

Cast: Hugh Buckler, Jimmie Savo, W.T. Stewart, Nancy Ann Hargreaves, Niles Welch, Brenda Bond, Monroe Owsley, Lewis Dayton, Laura O'Hara, Charles Esdale, Donald Hall, Louise Cardi

Notes: Pulled from Canadian theaters by end of December 1931. Never premiered officially in the USA.

* *Holiday*

Release date: July 1930

Director: Edward H. Griffith

Writers: Horace Jackson; based on the play *Holiday* by Philip Barry

Cinematography: Norbert Brodine

Production company: Pathé Exchange

Cast: Ann Harding, Mary Astor, Edward Everett Horton, Robert Ames, Hedda Hopper, Monroe Owsley, William Holden, Elizabeth Forrester, Mabel Forrest, Creighton Hale, Hallam Cooley, Mary Forbes

* *Kid the Kidder*

Release date: October 1930

Director: Ray McCarey

Writer: Paul Dickey

Production company: Pathé Exchange

Cast: Vera Marsh, Monroe Owsley, Emerson Treacy, Don Dillaway, Ray Cooke

Notes: Two reels short film. Probably lost.

* *Free Love*

Release date: December 1930

Director: Hobart Henley

Writers: Edwin H. Knopf, Winifred Dunn, Erwin Kelsey; based on the play *Half Gods* by Sidney Howard

Cinematography: Hal Mohr

Production company: Universal Pictures

Cast: Genevieve Tobin, Conrad Nagel, Monroe Owsley, Bertha Mann, Ilka Chase, George Irving, Reginald Pasch, ZaSu Pitts, Slim Summerville, Sidney Bracey

* *Ten Cents a Dance*

Release date: January 1931

Director: Lionel Barrymore

Writers: Jo Sterling and Dorothy Howell; based on the song "Ten Cents a Dance" with lyrics by Lorenz Hart and music by Richard Rodgers

Cinematography: Ernest Bakker and Gilbert Warrenton

Production company: Columbia Pictures

Cast: Barbara Stanwyck, Ricardo Cortez, Monroe Owsley, Sally Blane, Blanche Friderici, Martha Sleeper, David Newell, Victor Patel, Sidney Bracey, Abe Lyman and his orchestra, Aggie Herring, Harry Todd, Phyllis Crane, Olive Tell, Al Hill, Pat Harmon

* *Honor Among Lovers*

Release date: February 1931

Director: Dorothy Arzner

Writers: Gertrude Purcell and Austin Parker; based on the story by Austin Parker

Cinematography: George Foley

Production company: Paramount Pictures

Cast: Claudette Colbert, Frederic March, Monroe Owsley, Charles Ruggles, Ginger Rogers, Avon Taylor, Pat J. O'Brien, Janet McLeary, Ralph Morgan, Leonard Carey, Charles Halton, Granville Bates

* *Indiscreet*

Release date: May 1931

Director: Leo McCarey

Writers: Leo McCarey, Buddy G. DeSylva, Lew Brown, Ray Henderson; based on the story Obey That Impulse by DeSylva, Brown, and Henderson

Cinematography: Ray June and Gregg Toland

Production company: United Artists

Cast: Gloria Swanson, Ben Lyon, Arthur Lake, Barbara Kent, Monroe Owsley, Maude Eburne, Henry Kolker, Nella Walker

* *This Modern Age*

Release date: August 1931

Director: Nick Grinde

Writers: Frank Butler and Sylvia Thalberg; based on the story *Girls Together* by Mildred Cram

Cinematography: Charles Rosher

Production company: Metro-Goldwyn-Mayer

Cast: Joan Crawford, Pauline Frederick, Neil Hamilton, Monroe Owsley, Hobart Bosworth, Emma Dunn, Albert Conti, Adrienne D'Ambricourt, Marcelle Corday

Notes: Clarence Brown took over directing for the second version of *This Modern Age*.

* *Unashamed*

Release date: June 1932

Director: Harry Beaumont

Writer: Bayard Veiller

Cinematography: Nobert Brodine

Production company: Metro-Goldwyn-Mayer

Cast: Helen Twelvetrees, Robert Young, Lewis Stone, Jean Hersholt, John Miljan, Monroe Owsley, Robert Warwick, Gertrude Michael, Wilfred North, Tommy Jackson, Louise Beaver

Notes: Drew inspiration from the death of Francis Donaldson III.

* *Hat Check Girl*

Release date: September 1932

Director: Sidney Lanfield

Writer: Barry Conners and Philip Klein; based on the novel *Hat Check Girl* by Rian James

Cinematography: Glen MacWilliams

Production company: Fox Film Corporation

Cast: Sally Eilers, Ben Lyon, Monroe Owsley, Ginger Rogers, Noel Madison, Dewey Robinson, Arthur Pierson, Purnell Pratt, Harold Goodwin, Eulalie Jensen

* *Call Her Savage*

Release date: November 1932

Director: John Francis Dillon

Writers: Edward Burke; based on the novel *Call Her Savage* by Tiffany Thayer

Cinematography: Lee Garmes

Production company: Fox Film Corporation

Cast: Clara Bow, Gilbert Roland, Thelma Todd, Monroe Owsley, Estelle Taylor, Weldon Heyburn, Willard Robertson, Anthony Jowitt, Fred Kohler, Russell Simpson, Margaret Livingston, Carl Stockdale, Dorothy Peterson

* *The Keyhole*

Release date: March 1933
Director: Michael Curtiz
Writer: Robert Presnell, Sr.; based on the story *Adventuress* by Alice D.G. Miller
Cinematography: Barney McGill
Production company: Warner Bros. Pictures
Cast: Kay Francis, George Brent, Glenda Farrell, Monroe Owsley, Allen Jenkins, Helen Ware, Henry Kolker, Ferdinand Gottschalk, George Chandler

* *Ex-Lady*
Release date: April 1933
Director: Robert Florey
Writers: David Boehm; based on an unproduced play by Edith Fitzgerald and Robert Riskin
Cinematography: Barney McGill
Production company: Warner Bros. Pictures
Cast: Bette Davis, Gene Raymond, Kay Strozzi, Monroe Owsley, Ferdinand Gottschalk, Alphonse Ethier, Frank McHugh, Claire Dodd, Bodil Rosing
Notes: Remake of *Illicit* (1931).

* *Brief Moment*
Release date: September 1933
Director: David Burton
Writers: Edith Fitzgerald and Brian Marlow; based on the play *Brief Moment* by S.N. Behrman
Cinematography: Ted Tetzlaff
Production company: Columbia Pictures
Cast: Gene Raymond, Carole Lombard, Donald Cook, Monroe Owsley, Arthur Hohl, Irene Ware, Teresa Maxwell-Conover, Reginald Mason

* *The Woman Who Dared*

Release date: February 1934

Director: Millard Webb

Writers: Curtis Kenyon, King Guidice, Charles E. Roberts, Robert Webb

Cinematography: Robert E. Cline

Production company: William Berke Productions

Cast: Claudia Dell, Monroe Owsley, Lola Lane, Douglas Fowley, Robert Elliott, Matty Fain, Bryant Washburn, Eddie Kane, Esther Muir, Matthew Betz, Paul Fix, Sidney Tracey, Joseph W. Girard, Herbert Evans

Notes: Possibly lost. One print turned up in 2005, but it's currently unknown if it was salvageable.

* *Twin Husbands*

Release date: April 1934

Director: Frank R. Strayer

Writers: Robert Ellis and Anthony Coldeway

Cinematography: M.A. Anderson

Production company: Invincible Pictures

Cast: John Miljan, Shirley Grey, Monroe Owsley, Hale Hamilton, Robert Elliott, Maurice Black, William Franklin, Wilson Benge

* *Little Man, What Now?*

Release date: May 1934

Director: Frank Borzage

Writers: William Anthony McGuire; based on the novel *Little Man, What Now?* (*Kleiner Mann — was nun?*) by Hans Fallada

Cinematography: Norbert F. Brodin

Production company: Universal Pictures

Cast: Margaret Sullavan, Douglass Montgomery, Alan Hale, Catherine Doucet, DeWitt Jennings, G.P. Huntley, Muriel Kirkland, Fred Kohler, Mae Marsh, Donald Haines, Christian Rub, Alan Mowbray, Monroe Owsley

* *Wild Gold*

Release date: June 1934

Director: George Marshall

Writers: Lester Cole, Henry Johnson, Dudley Nichols, Lamar Trotti

Cinematography: Joseph A. Valentine

Production company: Fox Film Corporation

Cast: John Boles, Claire Trevor, Harry Green, Roger Imhof, Ruth Gillette, Monroe Owsley, Edward Gargan, Suzanne Kaaren, Wini Shaw, Blanca Vischer, Elsie Larson, Gloria Roy, Myrla Bratton

* *Shock*

Release date: July 1934

Director: Roy J. Pomeroy

Writers: Madeleine Ruthven and Roy J. Pomeroy

Cinematography: Jack MacKenzie

Production company: Monogram Pictures

Cast: Ralph Forbes, Gwenllian Gill, Monroe Owsley, Reginald Sharland, Mary Forbes, Douglas Walton, Billy Bevan, Clyde Cook, Alex Courtney, David Holt, Charles Coleman, David Dunbar, C. Montague Shaw, Eric Snowden, Olaf Hytten

* *She Was a Lady*

Release date: July 1934

Director: Hamilton MacFadden

Writers: Gertrude Purcell; based on the novel *She Was a Lady* by Elisabeth Cobb

Cinematography: Bert Glennon

Production company: Fox Film Corporation

Cast: Helen Twelvetrees, Donald Woods, Ralph Morgan, Monroe Owsley, Irving Pichel, Doris Lloyd, Kitty Kelly, Halliwell Hobbes, Mary Forbes, Jackie Searl, Barbara Weeks, Karol Kay, Paul Harvey, Harold Goodwin, Anne Howard

* *Behold My Wife!*

Release date: December 1934

Director: Mitchell Leisen

Writers: Grover Jones and Vincent Lawrence; based on the novel *The Translation of a Savage* by Sir Gilbert Parker

Cinematography: Leon Shamroy

Production company: Paramount Pictures

Cast: Sylvia Sidney, Gene Raymond, Laura Hope Crews, H.B. Warner, Juliette Compton, Monroe Owsley, Ann Sheridan, Charlotte Granville, Kenneth Thomson, Dean Jagger, Eric Blore, Charles Middleton, Rina De Liguoro

* *Rumba*

Release date: February 1935

Director: Marion Gering

Writers: Guy Endore and Howard J. Green

Cinematography: Ted Tetzlaff

Production company: Paramount Pictures

Cast: George Raft, Carole Lombard, Lynne Overman, Margo, Gail Patrick, Iris Adrian, Monroe Owsley, Jameson Thomas, Soledad Jimenez, Paul Porcasi, Samuel S. Hinds, Virginia Hammond

* *Goin' to Town*

Release date: May 1935

Director: Alexander Hall

Writer: Mae West

Cinematography: Karl Struss

Production company: Paramount Pictures

Cast: Mae West, Paul Cavanagh, Gilbert Emery, Marjorie Gateson, Tito Coral, Ivan Lebedeff, Fred Kohler, Monroe Owsley, Grant Withers, Luis Alberni, Lucio Villegas, Mona Rico, Wade Boteler, Paul Harvey, Joe Frye, Vladimar Bykoff

* *Remember Last Night?*

Release date: November 1935

Director: James Whale

Writers: Harry Clark, Doris Malloy, Dan Totheroh; based on the novel *Hangover Murders* by Adam Hobhouse

Cinematography: Joseph Valentine

Production company: Universal Pictures

Cast: Edward Arnold, Robert Young, Constance Cummings, George Meeker, Sally Eilers, Reginald Denny, Louise Henry, Gregory Ratoff, Robert Armstrong, Monroe Owsley, Jack La Rue, Edward Brophy, Gustav von Seyffertitz, Rafaela Ottiano, Arthur Treacher, E.E. Clive

* *Private Number*

Release date: June 1936

Director: Roy Del Ruth

Writers: William M. Conselman and Gene Markey; based on the play *Common Clay* by Cleves Kinkead

Cinematography: J. Peverell Marley

Production company: Twentieth Century-Fox Film Corporation

Cast: Loretta Young, Robert Taylor, Basil Rathbone, Patsy Kelly, Joe E. Lewis, Marjorie Gateson, Paul Harvey, Jane Darwell, Paul Stanton, John Miljan, Monroe Owsley, Billy Bevan, George Irving, May Beatty

Notes: Also based on the movie *Common Clay* (1930).

* *Yellowstone*

Release date: August 1936

Director: Arthur Lubin

Writers: Jefferson Parker, Stuart Palmer, Houston Branch; based on a story by Arthur Phillips

Cinematography: Milton R. Krasner

Production company: Universal Pictures

Cast: Henry Hunter, Judith Barrett, Andy Devine, Alan Hale, Ralph Morgan, Monroe Owsley, Rollo Lloyd, Raymond Hatton, Paul Harvey, Paul Fix, Michael Loring

* *Mr. Cinderella*

Release date: October 1936

Director: Edward Sedgwick

Writers: Richard Flournoy, Arthur V. Jones, Jack Jevne, Edward Sedgwick

Cinematography: Milton R. Krasner

Production company: Hal Roach Studios

Cast: Jack Haley, Betty Furness, Arthur Treacher, Raymond Walburn, Robert McWade, Rosina Lawrence, Monroe Owsley, Kathleen Lockhart, Edward Brophy, Charlotte Wynters, Tom Dugan, Iris Adrian, Toby Wing, Morgan Wallace, Arthur Aylesworth, John Hyams, Leila McIntyre

* *Hideaway Girl*

Release date: November 1936

Director: George Archainbaud

Writers: David Garth and Joseph Moncure March

Cinematography: George T. Clemens and Ted Tetzlaff

Production company: Paramount Pictures

Cast: Shirley Ross, Robert Cummings, Martha Raye, Monroe Owsley, Elizabeth Russell, Louis Da Pron, Ray Walker, Robert Middlemass, Edward Brophy, James Eagles, Bob Murphy, Lee Phelps, Kenneth Harlan, Jimmie Dundee

* *The Hit Parade*

Release date: April 1937

Director: Gus Meins

Writers: Bradford Ropes, Samuel Ornitz, Harry Ruskin

Cinematography: Ernest Miller

Production company: Republic Pictures

Cast: Frances Langford, Phil Regan, Max Terhune, Edward Brophy, Louise Henry, Pert Kelton, Pierre Watkins, J. Farrell MacDonald, Monroe Owsley, Inez Courtney, William Demarest, George Givot, Sammy White, Paul Garner, Sam Wolfe, Richard Hakins, Yvonne Manoff, Mildred Winston, Barbara Johnston, Carl Hoff and the Hit Parade Orchestra, Ivie Anderson, Duke Ellington and his orchestra, Eddy Duchin and his orchestra, Pat Padgett, Pick Malone, Al Pearce, Sayle Taylor, Ed Thorgersen, Ed "Oscar" Platt, Lou Fulton, Arlene Harris, Stanley Fields, Harvey Clark, Kathleen Howard

Notes: Original running time of eighty-three minutes. Republic later trimmed the film to sixty-seven minutes and reissued it as *I'll Reach for a Star*.

SOURCES

CHAPTER 1

1. "Owsley-Matthews." *The Atlanta Constitution,* 21 October 1880, p. 4 *newspapers.com*
2. "Opera For School Benefit." *St. Louis Globe-Democrat,* 1 March 1909, p. 38 *newspapers.com*
3. "Former Georgian Dies In California." *The Atlanta Constitution,* 16 July 1925, p. 16. *newspapers.com*
4. "$5000 If He Finishes Shooting by Christmas." *Exhibitors Herald-World,* 1 November 1930, p. 43. *Media History Digital Library.*
5. Aydelotte, Winifred. "Monroe Owsley Proves That He Has Vivid Imagination." *Los Angeles Evening Post-Record,* 13 June 1931, p. 7. *newspapers.com.*
6. Conner, B.U.L., Dr. "The Fence." *El Paso Herald-Post,* 10 August 1932. *fultonhistory.com.*
7. "Brother of El Pasoan Stage Hit In New York." *El Paso Times,* 20 January 1929, p. 17. *newspapers.com.*
8. Shipp, Cameron. "Last Notice For Buck Owsley." *The Charlotte News,* 13 June 1937, p. 26. *newspapers.com.*
9. Easton, Frank. "Her Boarding House Days." *Modern Screen,* 1 May 1936, p. 62. *Media History Digital Library.*
10. Blair, Harry N. "Call It Luck." *The New Movie Magazine,* April 1931, p. 79. *Media History Digital Library.*
11. Swindell, Larry. *Spencer Tracy: A Biography.* Coronet, 1974.
12. "Monroe Owsley Well Acquainted With Role He Plays at Victory." *The Dayton Herald,* 25 April 1925, p. 9. *newspapers.com.*
13. "Cohan Comedy Comes Tonight." *The State* [Columbia, South Carolina], 8 May 1923, p. 14. *newspapers.com.*
14. Blair, Harry N. "Call It Luck." *The New Movie Magazine,* April 1931, p. 79. *Media History Digital Library.*
15. "Stage Ambitions Of Monroe Owsley." *Hartford Courant,* 25 February 1924, p.7. *newspapers.com.*
16. "'40 Winks' Speedy." *The Morning Union* [Springfield, Massachusetts], 10 February 1925, p. 8. *newspapers.com.*
17. "Schubert-Teck—"The Goose Hangs High." *Buffalo Courier,* 23 September 1924, p. 5. *newspapers.com.*
18. Muir, James. "Stuart Walker Players." *Dayton Daily News,* 14 April 1925, p. 20. *newspapers.com.*
19. Powers, Murray. "Astor Developing Gramercy Park; Vanderbilt Planning

Steamship Line At Victory." *The Dayton Herald,* 21 April 1925, p. 11. *newspapers.com.*

20. "Stock Star Also Denies Engagement To Follies' Beauty—For Her Sake." *Dayton Daily News,* 3 May 1925, p. 17. *newspapers.com.*
21. "Cupid And The Show Girls." *The Washington Herald Sun,* 14 June 1925, p. 5. *newspapers.com.*
22. *Cincinnati Commercial Tribune,* 24 May 1925. *fultonhistory.com.*
23. "His Hope To Get Girl As Show Ends." *Dayton Daily News,* 19 June 1925, p. 40. *newspapers.com.*

CHAPTER 2

1. "Concerning Mr. Owsley." *New York Sun,* 10 April 1933. fultonhistory.com.
2. "The Poli Players Are Welcomed by Mayor Parker." *The Springfield Daily Republican,* 22 April 1926, p. 9. *newspapers.com.*
3. "Players Steps And Sing To 'Irene' Tune." *The Springfield Daily Republican,* 1 June 1926, p. 6. *newspapers.com.*
4. "Foster Williams In Elliott Nugent Role." *The Springfield Daily Republican,* 8 June 1926, p. 7. *newspapers.com.*
5. "Players in Musical Comedy in Which Busby Berkeley Stars and Monroe Owsley Is Life-Saver." *The Republican* [Springfield, Massachusetts], 13 July 1926, p. 9. *newspapers.com.*
6. West, James L.W. III; Daniel, Anne Margaret "Introduction." *The Great Gatsby: The 1926 Broadway Script.* Cambridge University Press, 2024, p.xxx.
7. Capon, Alan. "Trenton: Hollywood of the North." *The Kingston Whig-Standard,* 3 April 1992, p. 13. *newspapers.com.*
8. Blair, Harry N. "Call It Luck." *The New Movie Magazine,* April 1931, p. 79. *Media History Digital Library.*
9. Aydelotte, Winifred. "Monroe Owsley Proves That He Has Vivid Imagination." *Los Angeles Evening Post-Record,* 13 June 1931, p. 7. *newspapers.com.*

CHAPTER 3

1. Daly, Phil M. "Along the Rialto." *The Film Daily,* 14 October 1930, p. 4. *Media History Digital Library.*
2. Barry, Philip. *Holiday.* Samuel French, 2017, p. 106.
3. Pollock, Arthur. "The Theaters." *The Brooklyn Daily Eagle,* 27 November 1928, p. 40. *newspapers.com.*
4. Blair, Harry N. "Call It Luck." *The New Movie Magazine,* April 1931, p. 79. *Media History Digital Library.*
5. Daly, Phil M. "Along the Rialto." *The Film Daily,* 1 August 1930, p. 4. *Media History Digital Library.*
6. Astor, Mary. *A Life on Film.* Delacorte, 1971, p. 83.
7. Mook, S.R. "He's Sore Because He's A Hit." *Silver Screen,* October 1931, p.38.

Media History Digital Library.
8. Busby, Marquis. "Monroe Owsley Getting Tired of Being 'Villain'." *Albany Times-Union,* 14 June 1931. *fultonhistory.com.*
9. "Monroe Owsley To Stay With Lasky." *Los Angeles Times,* 11 November 1930. *fultonhistory.com.*
10. "'Free Love' At The Elisnore." *The Capital Journal* [Salem, Oregon], 18 February 1931, p. 11. *newspapers.com.*
11. Owsley, Monroe. "Hollywood Stimulates American Sightseeing." *The Film Daily,* 29 December 1930, p. 5. *Media History Digital Library.*
12. Smith, Ella. *Starring Miss Barbara Stanwyck.* Random House Publishing, 1985, p. 27.
13. Barrier, Herbert, Jr. "Actor Visits, Wants to Stay." *The Knoxville Journal,* 7 February 1933, p. 1.
14. Busby, Marquis. "Monroe Owsley Getting Tired of Being 'Villain'." *Albany Times-Union,* 14 June 1931. *fultonhistory.com.*
15. "Flying Actors." *Detroit Free Press,* 26 May 1931, p. 15. *newspapers.com.*
16. "Brief Reviews of Current Pictures." *Photoplay,* July 1931, p. 10. *Media History Digital Library.*

CHAPTER 4

1. "News and Gossip." *Motion Picture Magazine,* July 1931, p. 37. *Media History Digital Library.*
2. Albert, Katherine. "The Unknown Hollywood I Know." *Photoplay,* March 1932, p. 40. *Media History Digital Library.*
3. Shaffer, George. "Movie Gossip From Hollywood." *Chicago Tribune,* 19 June 1931, p. 23. *newspapers.com.*
4. Busby, Marquis. "Young Master Owsley Would Like to Be in On the Final Clinch." *Omaha Sunday Bee News,* 14 June 1931. *newspapers.com.*
5. "Passing In Review." *Motion Picture Herald,* 13 June 1931, p. 28. *Media History Digital Library.*
6. Muir, Florabel. "Joan Crawford Puts Scissors On 'Modern Age.'" *Daily News* [New York City, New York], 23 June 1931, p. 34. *newspapers.com.*
7. Starr, Jimmy. "Coveted Part To Loretta's Young Sister." *Los Angeles Evening Express,* 29 June 1931, p. 14. *newspapers.com.*
8. Carroll, Harrison. "Behind the Scene in Hollywood." *The Charlotte Observer,* 15 August 1931, p. 20. *newspapers.com.*
9. "Invention." *The Standard Union* [Brooklyn, New York], 19 June 1931, p. 11. newspapers.com.
10. Carroll, Harrison. "Behind the Scenes in Hollywood." *Kansas City Journal,* 6 October 1931, p. 14. *newspapers.com.*
11. Mook, S.R. "He's Sore Because He's A Hit." *Silver Screen,* October 1931, p.38. *Media History Digital Library.*
12. Wilson, Harry. "Queens." *Variety,* 8 October 1931, p. 45. *Media History Digital Library.*

13. "Hollywood Bandwagon." *The New Movie Magazine*, June 1932, p.121. *Media History Digital Library.*
14. Daniel, Frank. "Georgia's *Eleven* Movie Stars." *The Atlanta Journal*, 26 June 1932, p. 9. *newspapers.com.*
15. Merrick, Mollie. "Garbo to Make Three Films." *The Buffalo News*, 1 July 1932, p. 14. *newspapers.com.*
16. Moffitt, J.C. "Joan Gets Even For College Snub." *The Plain Dealer* [Cleveland, Ohio], 17 June 1932, p. 9. *newspapers.com.*
17. "News and Gossip of the Studios." *Motion Picture*, July 1932, p. 38. *Media History Digital Library.*
18. "News and Gossip." *Motion Picture*, May 1931, p. 116. *Media History Digital Library.*

CHAPTER 5

1. Shaffer, George. "Headlines Save Movies Cost Of Fanciful Plots." *Daily News* [New York City, New York], 13 June 1932, p. 32. *newspapers.com.*
2. Aliperti, Cliff. "Real-Life Society 'Honor Slaying' Inspires Two 1932 Films." *Immortal Ephemera*, 21 Sept. 2015, *immortalephemera.com/56204/honor-slaying-inspires-1932-movies.*
3. "Cinema: The New Pictures." *Time*, 25 July 1932. *time.com.*
4. "Legal Procedure Given Recognition." *The Montgomery Advertiser*, 14 August 1932, p. 23. *newspapers.com.*
5. Carroll, Harrison. "Behind the Scenes in Hollywood." *The Billings Gazette*, 16 August 1932, p. 4. *newspapers.com.*
6. "Night Club Escapades." *New York Times*, 8 October 1932. nytimes.com.
7. Wilson, Eleanore. "Hat Check Girl." *The Washington Daily News*, 24 September 1932, p. 15. *newspapers.com.*
8. *Picture Play Magazine*, 1933. *Media History Digital Library.*
9. James, Rian. "Reverting to Type." *The Brooklyn Daily Eagle*, 19 October 1932, p. 10. *newspapers.com.*
10. "MoMA Presents: Sidney Landfield's *Hat Check Girl*." 2014. *moma.org/calendar/film/1460.*
11. York, Cal. "Announcing The Monthly Broadcast of Hollywood Goings-On!" *Photoplay*, December 1932, p. 36. *Media History Digital Library.*
12. *"News and Gossip of the Studios." Motion Picture, January 1933, p. 30. Library of Congress*
13. Parsons, Louella. "Screen Getting Berkeley Square." *Tulsa World*, 13 December 1932, p. 9. newspapers.com.
14. Davis, Bette. *The Lonely Life: An Autobiography*, eBook, Hachette Books, 2017, ch. 9.
15. "'Rome Express' Excellent; 'Ex-Lady' For Flappers Only." *The Hollywood Reporter*, 7 February 1933, p. 5. *Media History Digital Library.*
16. Quirk, Lawrence J. *Fasten Your Seat Belts: The Passionate Life of Bette Davis*, William Morrow and Company, Inc., 1990, p. 79.

17. Quirk, Lawrence J. *Fasten Your Seat Belts: The Passionate Life of Bette Davis,* William Morrow and Company, Inc., 1990, p. 78.
18. "Concerning Mr. Owsley." *New York Sun,* 10 April 1933. *fultonhistory.com.*

CHAPTER 6

1. "Movie Actor Sued." *The Buffalo News,* 19 January 1933, p. 15. newspapers.com.
2. Luther, Betty. "He's Tired Of Playing The Cad." *El Paso Herald-Post,* 27 January 1933, p. 6. *newspapers.com.*
3. "Monroe Owsley, Screen Actor, Unrecognized on Streets Here." *Richmond Times-Dispatch,* 13 April 1933, p. 2. newspapers.com.
4. Luther, Betty. "He's Tired Of Playing The Cad." *El Paso Herald-Post,* 27 January 1933, p. 6. *newspapers.com.*
5. Barrier, Herbert Jr. "Actor Visits, Wants to Stay." *The Knoxville Journal,* p.1 & 4. newspapers.com.
6. "Movie Actors With $17,500 And No Change." *The World-News* [Roanoke, Virginia], 10 February 1933, p. 2. newspapers.com.
7. "Monroe Owsley, Screen Actor, Unrecognized on Streets Here." *Richmond Times-Dispatch,* 13 April 1933, p. 2. newspapers.com.
8. "Monroe Owsley Still Seeking 'The One Girl.'" *El Paso Herald-Post,* 18 April 1933, p. 5. *newspapers.com.*
9. "Hollywood Day By Day." *New Movie Magazine,* May 1933, p. 16. *Media History Digital Library.*
10. "Breach of Promise Suit Is Dismissed." *The San Bernardino County Sun,* 3 June 1933, p. 1. *newspapers.com.*
11. "Safeway Stores Stage Great Show at Stadium." *Hollywood Filmograph,* 28 October 1933, p. 3. *Media History Digital Library.*
12. Wilk, Ralph. "A Little from 'Lots.'" *The Film Daily,* 27 November 1933, p. 6. *Media History Digital Library.*
13. Hastings, Chris. "Lost Victorian films saved from destruction." *The Daily Telegraph* [UK], 3 April 2005. *telegraph.co.uk.*

CHAPTER 7

1. "The Low Down." *The Hollywood Reporter,* 26 January 1934, p. 2. *Media History Digital Library.*
2. "He Meant Business." *Battle Creek Enquirer,* 27 February 1934, p. 22. *newspapers.com.*
3. Parsons, Louella. "Monroe Owsley Engaged to Wed." *Syracuse Journal,* 14 April 1934. fultonhistory.com.
4. "Katherine Toberman Mum on Troth State." *Los Angeles Evening Citizen News,* 28 April 1934, p. 9. *newspapers.com.*

5. "Courts." *Hollywood,* May 1934, p. 46. *Media History Digital Library.*

CHAPTER 8

1. "Showmen's Reviews." *Motion Picture Herald,* 28 July 1934, p. 45. *Media History Digital Library.*
2. *"Lafayette Shows Nautical Talkie." The Buffalo News,* 16 November 1934, p. 33. *newspapers.com.*
3. "Monroe Owsley Not Fond Of Fan Mail." *The Springfield Daily Republican,* 8 July 1934, p. 30. *newspapers.com.*
4. "Reviews of the New Features and Shorts." *The Film Daily,* 22 August 1934, p. 4. *Media History Digital Library.*
5. "Mayfair Drama Real Life Story." *The Ottawa Journal,* 10 November 1934, p. 24. newspapers.com.
6. Melcher, E. de S. "Melcher and His Hollywood Diary." *The Evening Star* [Washington, D.C.], 15 June 1934, p. 6. *newspapers.com.*
7. "New Films." *The Boston Globe,* 17 August 1934, p. 22. *newspapers.com.*
8. "Chooses Film Heroes To Appeal To Women." *The Morning News* [Wilmington, Delaware], 23 May 1935, p. 18. *newspapers.com.*
9. Barry, Barbara. "On-The-Set Reviews." *The New Movie Magazine,* April 1935, p. 65. *Media History Digital Library.*
10. "Notes." *Turner Classic Movies,* accessed 2024, *tcm.com/tcmdb/title/76578/goin-to-town.*
11. "Film Actor Saves Friend From Fire." *The Oklahoma News,* 27 February 1935, p. 2. *newspapers.com.*
12. "Patients See Dentist Have Own Teeth Out." *The New York Sun,* 30 March 1935. *fultonhistory.com.*

CHAPTER 9

1. "Hollywood Day By Day." *The New Movie Magazine,* June 1935, p. 26. *Media History Digital Library.*
2. "Owsley to Enter Car in Indianapolis Race." *News-Pilot* [San Pedro, California], 23 March 1935, p. 9. *newspapers.com.*
3. Copps, Joe. "Insinger To Make 'Big Time' Racing Debut On May 30." *The Owensboro Messenger,* 2 May 1935, p. 9. *newspapers.com.*
4. "1935 Indianapolis 500." *GP Archive,* accessed 24 June 2024, gparchive.com/indianapolis-500/1935-indianapolis-500.
5. Nemo. "Hollywood Day By Day." *The New Movie Magazine,* July 1935, p. 29. *Media History Digital Library.*
6. "Topics For Gossip." *Silver Screen,* July 1935, p. 60. *Media History Digital Library.*
7. "Terror Stalks Set of Murder Film." *Brooklyn Daily Eagle,* 15 December 1935. *fultonhistory.com.*

8. Carroll, Harrison. "Behind the Scenes in Hollywood." *Wilkes-Barre Times Leader,* 7 September 1935, p. 2. *newspapers.com.*
9. *Carroll, Harrison. "Behind the Scenes in Hollywood." The Gaffney Ledger, 14 September 1935, p. 4. newspapers.com.*
10. Poff, Tip. "That Certain Party." *The Los Angeles Times,* 23 February 1936, p. 43. *newspapers.com.*
11. "Purely Personal." *Motion Picture Daily,* 4 March 1936, p. 3. *Media History Digital Library.*
12. "Mrs. Harry M. Owsley Succumbs In Hollywood." *Battle Creek Enquirer,* 16 March 1936, p. 2. *newspapers.com.*

CHAPTER 10

1. Nevin, Marion. "Stuart Erwin Signed For Appearance Tour." *Evening Vanguard* [Venice, California], 29 May 1936, p. 1. *newspapers.com.*
2. "'Yellowstone' Filmed Against Wonderful Background, Ready in August." *Great Falls Tribune,* 25 July 1936, p. 7. *newspapers.com.*
3. "Paul Fix, for First Time in His Sinister Career, Is Not Killed Off in Film." *The Morning Union* [Springfield, Massachusetts], 13 August 1936, p. 14. *newspapers.com.*
4. "Entertainment with Irritations." *Hollywood Spectator,* 21 November 1936, p. 16-17. *Media History Digital Library.*
5. "'Hideaway Girl,' a Comedy Featuring the Charm of Shirley Ross and the Blatancy of Martha Raye, Is the Attraction at the Newman." *The Kansas City Star,* 13 December, p. 51. *newspapers.com.*

CHAPTER 11

1. "Chatterbox." *The Los Angeles Times,* 22 November 1936, p. 6. newspapers.com.
2. Woods, Marjorie B. "These Couples Keep Marriage In Perpetual Valentine Stage." *The Washington Post,* 9 February 1947, p. 2S. *Internet Archive.*
3. Soares, André. "Anita Page: The Last Surviving Silent Film Star." *Alt Film Guide,* 22 Aug. 2007, *altfg.com/anita-page.*
4. "Harry M. Owsley Dies At Los Angeles Homes." *El Paso Times,* 8 May 1937, p. 8. *newspapers.com.*
5. "S.M. Officials Hide Death of Harlow Friend." *The Times* [San Mateo, California], 9 June 1937, p. 1. *newspapers.com.*
6. "Owsley Body Rushed South." *Redwood City Tribune,* 9 June 1937, p. 3. *newspapers.com.*
7. "S.M. Officials Hide Death of Harlow Friend." *The Times* [San Mateo, California], 9 June 1937, p. 1. *newspapers.com.*
8. "Death Calls Actor Owsley." *The Los Angeles Times,* 9 June 1937, p. 21. *newspapers.com.*

9. "Monroe Owsley Interred In Grave Beside Parents." *The Los Angeles Times*, 10 June 1937, p. 23. *newspapers.com.*
10. "Monroe Owsley Will Probated." *The Los Angeles Times*, 20 June 1937, p. 10. *newspapers.com.*
11. Shipp, Cameron. "Last Notice For Buck Owsley." *The Charlotte News*, 13 June 1937, p. 26. *newspapers.com*.
12. Sobol, Louis. "New York Cavalcade: Down Memory Lane." *The San Francisco Examiner*, 9 June 1947, p. 13. *newspapers.com.*

ABOUT THE AUTHOR

When not asking questions about Monroe Owsley, Chase Lloyd (they/them) writes romances under the pen name Chace Verity. You may contact them at chaselloyd@chaceverity.com.

www.ingramcontent.com/pod-product-compliance
Lightning Source LLC
Chambersburg PA
CBHW071531040426
42452CB00008B/980

* 9 7 8 1 7 7 5 0 6 2 6 6 0 *